The RV Cookbook

# The RV Cookbook

## Over 100 Quick, Easy, and Delicious Recipes to Enjoy on the Road

**Amy Boyer and Daniella Chace**

THREE RIVERS PRESS • NEW YORK

Published by Three Rivers Press, New York, New York. Member of the Crown Publishing Group, a division of Random House, Inc.
www.crownpublishing.com

THREE RIVERS PRESS and the Tugboat design are registered trademarks of Random House, Inc.

Originally published by Prima Publishing, Roseville, California, in 2002.

Interior design by Melanie Haage.

Printed in the United States of America

**Library of Congress Cataloging-in-Publication Data**
Boyer, Amy.
The RV cookbook : over 100 quick, easy, and delicious recipes to enjoy on the road / Amy Boyer and Daniella Chace
p.    cm.
Includes index.
1. Cookery. 2. Mobile home living. I. Chace, Daniella. II. Title.
TX840.M6B68    2002
641.5'75—dc21                              2002070442
ISBN 0-7615-1495-3

10 9 8 7 6 5

First Edition

To my husband and best friend, Dean, who has
helped make my life a wonderful adventure!
—AMY

To my sweet G for your creativity
and enthusiasm in the kitchen.
—DANIELLA

# Contents

# Acknowledgments

## General Support and Encouragement
Jim Banholzer
Lois Wismer and Lowell Bishop
Vivienne and Dave Blythe
Bobbie and Dick Boyer
Eric Boyer
Darcie Chace
Katie and Tony Chace
Jo Jo and Ryan Cowan
Kim Eberbach
Joanne Edmondson
Merrilee and Tom Gomez
"Pancake" Tom Grundy
The Guyton Family
LaMar Harrington
Laura Higdon
Uri Johndrow
Linda Landkammer
Tudor McCook
Julie Mermelstein
Tara Hubbard and Eric Moulton
Nels Moulton
John Oblanas
Feli Funke-Reihle
Wolf Reihle
Gisela Salum
Gina Calderone and Marty Trumbore

## Supportive Folks at Our Favorite Kitchen Equipment Companies

Gretchen Holt at OXO
Janet Lampa at Zyliss

## Creative Recipe Contributors

Brandon "Gator" Anderson
Jim Banholzer
Vivienne Blythe
Bobbie Boyer
Gary Boyer
Joanne Brand
Katie Chace
Joan Gilbert
Jeffrey Guyton
Dean and Wendy Hagin
Dean Hernandez
Lynn McCarthy
Karim Merchant
John Oblanas

## Assistance

Amanda Jones of Extreme Motor Sports
The fish guys at the Atkinsons' Markets

## Publishing Staff

Denise Sternad, Michelle McCormack, and the whole creative crew at Prima Publishing

## Taste Testing and Loving Support

Gary Boyer
Dean Hernandez
Four-legged critters Pip, Caledonia, Trout, Sailor, Milo, and Harold; Marco, Batty, Rudy, and Hacket

# Introduction

The call of the open road beckons more and more of us to seek the adventure of RV travel. This book, however, though directed to RV users, does not have to be limited to RV cooking. It's very handy for small-apartment dwellers or anyone with a small cooking space. But if you have purchased, borrowed, or been given this book, chances are you have chosen to heed the call and join the millions of folks who have made RVing a part of their lives. Whether you are traveling by RV for a week, a month, or a lifetime, we encourage you to embrace the spirit of exploration! Enjoy each new vista, welcome each new day, and create your very own journey. There's so much to see and experience in your home on wheels!

While you're out there enjoying life, we want you to eat well too! We have created this cookbook for those of you who would like to prepare delicious meals, whether you're in the middle of an RV park or the middle of the Mojave Desert. Creating satisfying meals doesn't have to be complicated—it simply requires a bit of planning. We have developed and tested more than 100 recipes to please your palate without cramping your style and have included tips and guidelines that will help keep your RV kitchen organized and running smoothly. Life is an adventure—enjoy it!

# CHAPTER 1

# Extraordinary Equipment

## Tools and Tips for an Efficient Kitchen

 Always have your RV ready to go! Keep it stocked with its own set of versatile and efficient equipment and tools.

- Antiskid mat for refrigerator, drawers, closets, etc.
- Bag clips for sealing opened bags of chips and snacks
- Baking pans, muffin pan, and cookie tray (nonstick, air-pocket trays resist burning)
- Barbecue tongs, spatula, and fork
- Bottle opener (look for one that works on bottles, twist caps, beverage cans, and jars)
- Boxes for sorting food (Plastic tubs are lightweight and unbreakable, and they stack well. The see-through variety makes it easy to access what you're looking for.)

- Can opener (look for one with an easy-grip handle)
- Charcoal and lighter
- Cloth napkins (they reduce paper waste and are festive)
- Coffeemaker or French press
- Colander or salad spinner (a thick interior strainer from a salad spinner can double as a colander—look for one that is tough enough to strain pasta as well)
- Cooking utensils, including a large serving spoon, spatula, pasta spoon, ladle, and slotted spoon (Look for easy-grip rubber-handled utensils that can be purchased in most kitchen stores. The rubber and soft plastic material keep them quiet in drawers even while you're driving.)
- Corkscrew or wine bottle opener (buy the smallest efficient opener you can find)
- Cutting board with nonskid backing (Choose either rigid plastic or roll-up flexible plastic, depending on your storage space. Buy three and use one exclusively for fish and meat products; another for garlic, onions, and other foods with strong flavors; and the third for fruits, breads, and other foods with delicate flavors. This way you won't mix flavors and you won't risk spreading salmonella or other microorganisms from fish and meat products.)
- Divider tray for silverware (keeps silverware organized and reduces noise while you're driving)
- Fire extinguisher (keep this within reach and make sure everyone knows where it is)

- Fire starter sparker
- Food chopper (look for one with an attached con-tainer to eliminate the need for a cutting board)
- Frying pan, large, with lid (get one with two handles for easier nesting)
- Garlic press
- Grater, for cheese and cold butter (look for one that supports itself in a bowl and has an easy-grip handle)
- Ice cube trays (look for ones with thin covers so you can stack another tray or packaged food on top of it)
- Knives with covers, such as bread, paring, and chef's knives
- Matches, long
- Measuring cups, adjustable or individual (look for ones that save space and can be used for both wet and dry ingredients)
- Measuring spoons (adjustable or nesting spoons take up less room)
- Mixing bowls, one large and one small, preferably nesting (look for ones with antiskid bottoms)
- Paper towels and holder (Under-the-counter or under-cupboard holders are available. Either use paper towels sparingly or use cloth towels and sponges for cleanup.)
- Pepper mill, for fresh ground pepper
- Pie pan
- Pressure cooker

- Rubber bands
- Saucepans, large and medium, with lids (these can double as mixing bowls)
- Scissors
- Serving dish, small serving bowls for dips, etc.
- Silicone spatula (look for heat-resistant spatulas—they last longer and won't leach chemicals into your food)
- Skewers (metal or bamboo) for grilling
- Spice mills (look for mixed spices in jars with a grinder top)
- Spices in jars or bags, plus a tray to hold them (you can save and reuse small bottles with screw-on lids)
- Spray oil bottle (These empty spray bottles are sold at kitchen stores. Just add your own oil. You'll use less oil when spraying it rather than pouring it on.)
- Trivet and pot holders (kitchen towels can double as pot holders in a pinch)
- Vegetable peeler (or leave skins on for extra nutrients)
- Whisk (A small whisk is usually big enough unless you are cooking for large groups.)
- Whistling teapot (It's easy to forget that you have water boiling when you are on the road and out of a normal routine. Whistles are a safe and fun way to remind yourself when your water is ready.)
- Wine bottle stopper (look for one that fits all bottles and keeps wine fresh)

## Storage and Picnic Supplies

- Bag clips or clothespins
- Heavy-duty aluminum foil
- Mesh bags for hanging produce
- Paper plates and cups and plastic silverware (don't throw out plastic silverware—reuse it instead)
- Plastic containers with lids
- Plastic wrap
- Sealable bags in quart and gallon sizes
- Thermos
- Water bottles for hikes

## Personal Equipment

- Coffee mugs (choose travel mugs that fit in your RV's drink holders)
- Dinner plates
- Glasses or plastic cups for each family member
- Salad, soup, cereal bowls
- Silverware

## Additional Items

These are items not necessary for a fully functioning kitchen, but they're nice to have if you have space for them.

- Blender (comes in handy for making smoothies, summer drinks, and pudding)
- Cooler (extra) for overflow produce, picnics, large group activities, etc.

- Crock Pot

- Dish drain rack

- Food processor

- Hibachi

- Microwave

- Pan for grilling (Grilling pans have small holes that allow the heat to cook the food but keep small chopped vegetables from falling through the grill. Nonstick pans are easy to clean.)

- Pyrex microwavable dishes

- Spice rack (in-drawer, wall mount, or freestanding)

- Tablecloth (vinyl, with weights), or attach small rocks with rubber bands to the corners of the tablecloth

- Toaster oven

## Cleaning Supplies

- Baking soda (a versatile and basic inexpensive deodorizer and cleaner)

- Dish soap (use a biodegradable product)

- Dish towels

- Dust pan and brush

- Pot scraper (little wedges of plastic that help clean up pans quickly, so less water is needed for scrubbing)

- Scrubber sponge

- Toothbrush (for cleaning hard-to-reach places, molding, and stove tops where grime collects)

## Indispensable Tips for Easy Cleanup

- Use as few chemical cleaners as possible, and you'll have a less toxic kitchen space and save money too.

- Clean countertops with baking soda and water.

- Since cutting boards can pick up the smells and flavors of garlic, onions, and fish, for example, use baking soda sprinkled on a damp sponge to clean the board, then follow with a rub of lemon juice to eliminate odors.

- Clean drains by pouring 1 cup baking soda and 1 cup vinegar into the drain and waiting for a few minutes. Follow up with a few quarts of boiling water. Drain cleaners are very toxic to breathe and toxic to the environment as they leave your drain and enter the water system.

- Make cleaning your grills easier by oiling them lightly with a vegetable oil such as organic canola oil before use.

- To get rid of the odors microwave ovens can pick up, place the juice of 1 lemon in a bowl of water in the microwave and heat it for up to two minutes. Your microwave will be refreshed!

- Remove mold and mildew with a paste of equal parts vinegar and salt.

- Purchase and use only nontoxic cleaners.

- Refer to the manuals that came with your RV's appliances and your cooking equipment for the manufacturers' recommended cleaning methods.

- Use toothpicks to dislodge small particles from stove nooks and hard-to-reach places.

# CHAPTER 2

# The Quick Getaway

## Tips for a Weekend Trip

 Short RV trips can be a wonderful way to reju-
venate and escape from the routines of day-to-
day life. In order for you to make your getaway
quick, easy, and stress-free, there are some things you
can do ahead of time to help make things run smoothly.

## Stocking the RV

Keep your RV stocked with all the essential tools you'll
need when you're on the road. Having a separate set of all
kitchen equipment that stays in the RV takes the guesswork
out of what to bring for each trip. You'll save time and you
won't have to worry about forgetting an important piece of
cookware.

You can also keep the RV stocked with food items such as spices, canned goods, and other nonperishables. If you're concerned about food spoilage due to rodents or subzero winter temps, you can keep these items stored in a box in a closet at home and restock your pantry just before your trip.

## GROCERY SHOPPING

Plan your meals for the short time you'll be away and shop ahead of time for items you'll need. You know your own grocery store at home better than any store you'll find on the road, so shopping will be quicker and easier.

## Food Preparation

You can do quite a bit of meal preparation well in advance of your weekend getaway. A few hours of planning ahead will free up valuable time once you're at your destination. Here are a few simple tips:

- Plan your meals ahead of time.

- Marinate fish and meat in resealable bags and freeze. You'll simply need to pull the bags from the freezer as you head out the door.

- Wash all produce at home. You can prechop vegetables for specific meals and store them in airtight containers, which will save lots of prep time later on.

- Precook pasta and rice for quick and easy stir-fries and main meals.

- Bake potatoes at home and then reheat for dinner or panfry for breakfast.

- Keep a few preseasoned boxed grain mixes (such as tabouli, couscous, or rice pilaf) handy for a quick and easy addition to your main meals.

- Mix together the dry ingredients for pancakes, waffles, pizza dough, cookies, breads, or brownies ahead of time in large resealable bags. Bring along oil, eggs, or other needed ingredients, and you can whip together homemade comfort foods without bowls or much cleanup.

- Keep it simple. A weekend getaway is an opportunity for you to relax and enjoy each moment!

# CHAPTER 3

# Secrets to Shopping

## Finding RV-Friendly Foods Anywhere

Whether you're living in an RV or a house, shopping for food is one of the inevitable chores of life. With a little planning and a bit of organization, this chore can be minimized, allowing you more time to enjoy your adventure and free time.

## Stocking the Pantry

Consider the food items you keep in your kitchen at home. You most likely have a variety of staple pantry items that either get used a lot or hardly at all. For example, if you use sugar in your coffee, you keep a supply of it handy for day-to-day use. How about baking soda and baking powder? Unless you bake a lot, these items tend to sit for months at a time, yet they are ready for you when you need them.

Now consider the storage limitations in your RV. Chances are, you don't have as much room in your RV as you do in your kitchen at home. So what's the solution? There are two basic rules of thumb:

1. Minimize quantities

2. Store them efficiently

Instead of storing a whole box of baking soda, transfer it to a smaller container. Rather than trying to find room for an entire bag of flour if you only plan to use a cup now and then, transfer a portion of it into a small sealable bag or storage container.

Here are some pantry items you'll need to have on hand for creating recipes in this book. Please don't be discouraged at the length of the list—it's simply a guideline. Remember that you may only need to stock the pantry with small quantities of some of these items. Check listed recipe ingredients and supplement your pantry as needed with specialty and bulk food items.

## Pantry Items

- Baking powder
- Baking soda
- Balsamic vinegar
- Black and Greek olives
- Black pepper
- Bread crumbs
- Bread, bagels, English muffins

- Brown sugar
- Canned items (vegetables, beans, fruit, tuna, chicken)
- Canned or boxed broth and soups
- Cocoa powder
- Crackers
- Dried beans, dried lentils, dehydrated bean flakes
- Flour (preferably unbleached whole wheat)
- Herbal tea, black tea, green tea, coffee
- Herbs, spices, spice blends (Italian seasoning, curry powder, chili powder, pumpkin pie spice, powdered ginger, powdered garlic, cinnamon, paprika, dry mustard, onion powder, Cajun seasoning, etc.)
- Honey
- Instant tapioca
- Molasses
- Nuts, seeds
- Olive oil, canola oil, spray oil
- Onions, potatoes, garlic
- Pancake mix (whole grain mix)
- Pasta, rice, couscous
- Potato flakes
- Powdered milk
- Raisins, dried fruit
- Sea salt
- Sugar (preferably unrefined turbinado sugar)

- Tomato sauce, tomato paste
- Tortilla shells
- Vanilla and almond extracts
- Whole oats (not instant)

# Refrigerator Items

Stock your RV refrigerator with daily staples and condiments that need to stay cool. Whenever possible, purchase items that have already been chilled at the grocery store, as this will greatly reduce the energy demands on your RV fridge. Try not to overfill the refrigerator, as good air circulation is necessary for its efficient functioning. Here are some items you will need to keep on hand for creating recipes in this book:

- Balsamic vinegar
- Butter
- Condiments (ketchup, Dijon mustard, steak sauce, Szechwan hot sauce, sesame oil, Worcestershire sauce, red curry paste, horseradish)
- Cream cheese
- Eggs
- Fresh fruits and vegetables
- Grated Parmesan cheese
- Lemon juice (fresh or bottled)
- Maple syrup
- Mayonnaise

- Milk or soy milk (or use powdered milk)
- Miscellaneous cheeses
- Nut butter (peanut, cashew, almond, etc.)
- Orange juice (fresh or frozen)
- Minced garlic (sold in a jar)
- Tamari or soy sauce

## Freezer Items

Use your freezer for storing frozen vegetables, meats, fish, juice, ice cubes, puff pastry, and so on.

## Additional Storage Tips

You may find that you don't have enough room in your refrigerator to store fresh produce. Consider purchasing an insulated cooler for these bulky items. It can double as an extra seat and will provide easy access to fruits and vegetables for both snacking and cooking.

Mesh bags provide an excellent storage area for potatoes, onions, and other produce that doesn't require refrigeration. Suspend a mesh bag from a wall or ceiling in your rig where there is good air circulation. You may need to stow the bag when you're on the move, but when you're parked, it'll keep produce handy yet out of the way.

Repackage spices into small containers or plastic resealable bags for easier storage. Label them and group them according to use: baking spices, herbs, seasoning salts, and so on.

# Finding Quality Food on the Road

Grocery shopping may seem like a daunting task when you're in an unfamiliar place. But, if you allow it to be part of your adventure, it shouldn't be too overwhelming. Here are some ideas to help add some fun to your shopping experiences.

## GROCERY STORES

Grocery stores across the country are filled with an amazing diversity of high-quality foods. You can shop for fresh produce in Aisle 1 and find culinary delights from around the world in Aisle 5! Turn your grocery-shopping forays into an extension of your adventure by taking the time to discover new foods and products. Try something new! Take a chance on something unknown and unfamiliar, and you just might discover a new favorite food. Allow yourself the freedom to experiment—it's a great way to turn meal preparation into a creative venture. (See Resources for a list of some of our favorite stores.)

## NATURAL FOOD STORES

Many natural food stores stock bulk foods in self-serve bins. You can buy as little or as much as you want, giving you the freedom to try some new foods without worrying about waste. Buying in bulk is much less expensive than buying packaged foods. You'll also find spices and teas in the bulk department of these stores at a fraction of the packaged prices. Especially well suited to the RV lifestyle, dehydrated soups, beans, potatoes, and mixes are easy to store and prepare. Please refer to the Natural Food Store list in the Resources for some of our favorite stores in your vicinity.

## ROADSIDE STANDS

Roadside stands not only provide the traveler with a great way to stock up on local produce, but they offer a glimpse of the locals as well. When you take the time to make a quick stop, you'll often come away with more than just fruit, vegetables, and the occasional apple pie—you'll have a better sense of the residents and their community as well.

## "PICK-YOUR-OWN" ORCHARDS

A fun way to get some exercise, fresh air, and a bushel of apples (or pears, peaches, blueberries, or strawberries . . .) is to spend the day at a farm that allows you to pick your own. You can join a group of friends and make a social event out of it! A day of picking fresh strawberries with friends can turn into an evening of fresh strawberry daiquiris!

## LOCAL MICROBREWERIES AND WINERIES

In your travels, plan to stop occasionally for a taste of the local brews and wines. Plan ahead though—a day of tasting shouldn't be immediately followed by hours of driving! You may want to pick up a few bottles of wine or beer to take with you for future imbibing.

## ALONG THE COAST

When your travels take you to the coast, ask the locals where they buy their seafood. You'll find that the freshest seafood is often available right off the boat. Make the most of your seafood "catch" and take the day to enjoy the sights and sounds of the harbor.

## REGIONAL FARE

"When in Rome, do as the Romans do . . ." and likewise, when you're in areas of the country known for their distinctive regional foods and dishes, have a taste! The Southwest is famous for its Mexican dishes, the Southeast is known for its Cajun cooking, and Pennsylvania for its authentic Pennsylvania Dutch cuisine. While in the Canadian Maritime provinces, be sure to sample the fresh seafood such as lobster in Nova Scotia. Enjoy the variety each area is famous for!

## HIGH-ALTITUDE COOKING

When traveling at higher altitudes, remember that water and other liquids boil at a lower temperature and cooking time may need to be increased to get the results you expect. Longer cooking times usually mean you'll need to increase the liquid in each dish. Add 1 to 2 tablespoons more liquid to each recipe when you are at 3,000 feet, 2 to 4 tablespoons at 5,000 feet, and 3 to 4 tablespoons at 7,000 feet. After making just a few recipes at high altitude, you'll have the system down and you can enjoy delicious hot meals with your gorgeous mountain vistas.

# CHAPTER 4

# Hearty Breakfasts

 When you start your day with a nutritious
breakfast, you'll have the energy for the day's
adventures that lie ahead. Fuel your body and
wake up your senses—it's a new day!

# Spiced Hearty Oatmeal

1 cup whole oats
1 cup nonfat or lowfat milk or soy milk
1 teaspoon pumpkin pie spice
1/2 teaspoon powdered ginger
1 tablespoon honey
1 tablespoon butter

In a small saucepan, mix the oats with the milk and cook over medium heat for 5 minutes, stirring occasionally. Add the remaining ingredients and blend well. Cover with a lid, turn off heat, and allow to sit for 2 minutes. Stir well and serve immediately.

**Serves 2.**

## Variations

Slice half an apple and throw in a handful of raisins and cook them along with the oats, or top bowls of oatmeal with banana slices or strawberries. Raisins are a great source of iron, a nutrient especially important for women.

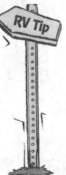

There's nothing quite like the taste of fresh berries, especially when you've picked them yourself! In your travels, keep your eyes open for berry bushes alongside the road. Some of the best berries are found where you least expect them.

# Potato Pancakes

Cooking spray
1 bag (16 ounces) hash browns, thawed
4 eggs, lightly beaten
1 cup pancake mix
1/2 teaspoon sea salt
1/2 teaspoon black pepper

Coat a large skillet with cooking spray and place over medium heat. Meanwhile, in a large mixing bowl, combine the hash browns, eggs, pancake mix, salt, and pepper. Stir well. Drop potato mixture by large spoonfuls into skillet. Cook over medium heat until browned, flipping once. Serve hot.

**Makes 12 pancakes.**

Use whole grain pancake mix such as Bob's Red Mill, which is available in most chain grocery stores. Buy organic hash browns when possible. Cascadian Farm brand hash browns can be found in the freezer section of many markets.

# Crisp French Toast

Cooking spray
4 eggs
1/2 teaspoon cinnamon
1/2 teaspoon real vanilla extract
1/4 cup sesame seeds
6 slices bread
Butter
2 to 6 tablespoons pure maple syrup

Coat a skillet with cooking spray and place over medium heat. Meanwhile, mix the eggs, cinnamon, vanilla, and sesame seeds in a flat pan such as a pie dish. Whip together with a fork or wire whisk. Coat each piece of bread in the egg batter and place in the skillet. Cook both sides of each piece of bread in the skillet until browned. Serve hot with butter and syrup.

**Serves 3 to 4.**

### Variations

Add fresh-grated nutmeg or wheat germ to the egg batter.

Add a tablespoon of water or milk to the batter to help it fluff up and mix well.

New England is famous for its sugar maple trees and the delicious, rich maple syrup that is produced from their sap. If your travels take you through Vermont, be sure to pick up a bottle of this pure, natural syrup and enjoy it on all your favorite breakfast treats.

**RV Tip**

**Nutrition Tip**

Use whole grain bread rather than white bread for a healthier version of this tasty classic recipe.

# Ba-Egg-les

1 bagel (with a large hole in the center)
1 egg
Spray oil or pat of butter
Dash sea salt
Dash pepper

Split the bagel in half. Whisk the egg in a small bowl. Soak each half of the bagel facedown in egg for 30 seconds. Coat a pan with spray oil or a pat of butter and heat. Place the bagel halves facedown in the pan and cook over medium heat for 5 minutes, turning twice. At the end of the cooking time, with the bagel halves facedown, pour the remainder of the egg into the center hole and cook another minute. Sprinkle with salt and pepper and serve hot.

**Serves 1.**

## Variations

If you like the sweeter variety of bagels (blueberry, cinnamon raisin, etc.), a drizzle of honey or maple syrup after cooking is a real treat.

If you prefer the savory bagel flavors (onion, garlic, etc.), add a slice of any cheese at the end of cooking and cover with a lid. You'll have a delicious melted cheese-egg bagel!

Nutrition Tip

Buy whole grain bagels—
they will give you long-
lasting energy for your
day.

# "Hailey's" Comet

1/4 cup chopped smoked turkey
1 tablespoon olive oil
4 eggs
1 teaspoon water or milk
3 scallions, chopped
1 tomato, chopped
3 tablespoons grated cheese

Sauté the meat in a pan with oil for 5 minutes to brown. Meanwhile, scramble the eggs in a bowl with the water or milk and scallions, then pour over the turkey. Stir occasionally, cooking about 4 minutes. Fold in the tomato and cheese and continue cooking until the cheese is melted.

**Serves 2.**

### Variations

Replace smoked turkey with leftover grilled meats, soy sausage, or whatever you have handy in the fridge.

Add herbs such as basil or dill to the egg batter.

Use several cheeses, such as Cheddar, smoked Gouda, or Swiss, to give this dish more depth.

If you're a real gourmet and have the time, top this dish with hollandaise sauce for a very special breakfast.

# Italian Omelet

1 small onion, minced
1 tablespoon olive oil
1/2 cup chopped or sliced black olives
1/4 cup chopped red pepper
1 small tomato, chopped
1/2 teaspoon Italian seasoning
4 eggs
Dash sea salt
Dash pepper
1/2 cup shredded mozzarella cheese

In a large frying pan, sauté the onion in olive oil until lightly browned. Add the olives, pepper, tomato, and Italian seasoning and cook over medium heat for 2 to 3 minutes. Remove from the pan and set aside on a plate. Whisk the eggs in a small bowl. Pour the eggs into the heated frying pan and cook over medium heat, lifting the edges of the egg to allow the uncooked egg to run underneath. When the egg is cooked, turn heat to low. Spread the sautéed vegetables evenly over the egg and sprinkle with salt and pepper. Top your omelet with mozzarella cheese. Leave the omelet unfolded and cover the pan with a lid. Cook over low heat for 1 to 2 minutes, until the cheese has melted. Cut the omelet in half and serve open-faced.

**Serves 2.**

# Breakfast Burritos

1/2 onion, sliced
8 Greek Kalamata olives, pitted and chopped
1 tablespoon olive oil
3 eggs
2 tablespoons grated Cheddar cheese
2 flour tortillas
Salsa (optional)

Sauté the onion and olives in olive oil in a skillet over medium heat for about 5 minutes. Scramble the eggs in a bowl and pour over the sautéed onion and olives. Cook for about 3 minutes. Top with the cheese and scramble. Continue cooking for 1 to 2 more minutes, until the cheese has melted. Divide the egg mixture into 2 servings and place on the tortillas. Top with salsa if desired and eat while hot.

**Serves 2.**

### Variations

Substitute black olives for the Kalamata olives, but remember the Kalamata olives have a sweeter flavor.

Add herbs such as basil or dill to the eggs for a richer flavor.

Add a teaspoon of water or milk to the eggs when whisking to produce lighter, fluffier cooked eggs. Toast the tortillas in a toaster oven or warm in a dry, clean skillet before topping with the eggs.

# Easy Banana-Spice Muffins

3 very ripe bananas (organic when possible)
1/4 cup orange juice
1/2 cup olive oil or butter, at room temperature
1/2 cup brown sugar
2 cups unbleached flour
1/2 teaspoon salt
1/2 teaspoon baking powder
1/2 teaspoon baking soda
4 teaspoons pumpkin pie spice

Preheat the oven to 375 degrees F. In a large bowl, mash the bananas and mix with the orange juice, oil or butter, and brown sugar. In a second bowl, mix the flour, salt, baking powder, baking soda, and spice together with a whisk. Add the dry ingredients to the wet and mix well. Spoon into a muffin pan (use 10 muffin cups for larger muffins, 12 for smaller muffins) and bake for 30 minutes. Eat warm, or store in a sealable bag to keep the muffins moist and fresh.

**Makes 10 large muffins or 12 small muffins.**

### Variations

Substitute 1/2 cup applesauce for 1/2 cup banana.

Add 1/2 to 1 cup raisins to mix.

Add 1/2 cup chopped nuts.

Put slices of bananas inside each muffin's batter before baking.

Use a muffin pan with paper or foil liners for easy cleanup.

Add 1/2 cup fresh ground flaxseed to the batter to add healthy oils and fiber. Use a coffee grinder to grind whole flaxseed into a powder. Ground flaxseed can be stored in plastic bags or containers in a cool dry place such as the freezer for weeks. Whole wheat flour works just as well as unbleached wheat flour in this recipe.

# Spicy Potato and Herbed Egg Scramble

1 can (15 ounces) sliced white potatoes
2 tablespoons olive oil
1 medium onion, coarsely chopped
1/4 teaspoon cayenne pepper
4 eggs, whisked
1 teaspoon Italian seasoning
Dash sea salt
Dash pepper

In a large saucepan, cook the potatoes in olive oil for 10 minutes over medium heat. Cover as needed to avoid splattering of oil. After 10 minutes, add the onion and cayenne pepper, mixing well. Cook another 5 minutes, until the onions are browned. Turn heat to low. Add the whisked eggs and Italian seasoning and stir until the mixture is well blended. Cover with a lid and heat on low for 5 minutes. Remove the lid and sprinkle the mixture with salt and pepper. Spoon onto plates and serve hot.

**Serves 2.**

## Variation

After adding the eggs, cook on low for 4 minutes, then add 1/2 cup of the shredded cheese of your choice. Cover with a lid and heat an additional minute. Delicious!

If you don't have a lid that's big enough to cover one of your larger pans or skillets, use heavy-duty aluminum foil. Simply pull out a sheet large enough to cover the pan and crimp it around the edges. If you don't want to fully cover the pan but need protection against splattering oil, simply poke holes in the foil. The steam will be able to escape, but not the oil.

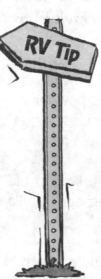

# All-Day Pancakes

*This high-protein version of the American classic breakfast is so healthy you could make it for breakfast, lunch, or dinner and satisfy that pancake craving any time of day.*

2 cups whole wheat flour
1/2 cup nonfat milk powder
4 teaspoons baking powder
1 teaspoon salt or sea salt
1/4 cup organic canola oil
1/4 cup water
1/2 cup blueberries, 1/2 cup blackberries, 1/4 cup ground flaxseed, or 1/2 teaspoon vanilla extract (optional)
Cooking spray

Combine the flour, milk powder, baking powder, and salt in a bowl and mix well. Add the oil and water and mix well. Fold in any optional ingredients, such as fresh berries, that you desire. Spray a skillet with cooking spray and place over medium heat until hot. Pour the batter into the skillet, cooking both sides until golden brown. (Or make fun shapes like snowflake patterns by filling a large, sturdy sealable bag with batter, then squeezing it out of a small hole snipped off the corner onto a hot skillet.) Serve hot with butter and maple syrup, nut butters, honey, or apple-sauce.

**Serves 2 to 4.**

Make this batter in advance and store it for several days until you need it, so you can sleep in late and have pancakes made in a jiffy. Wet batter stores for about three days in a well-sealed container in the refrigerator. Or mix the dry ingredients and store the mix in a plastic bag in the freezer for months. If you store a dry batch in a gallon-size sealable bag, you can add the wet ingredients directly to the bag, shake it up, and just snip the corner to squeeze directly onto a skillet. No bowls to clean when you're done!

If you don't have baking powder, add 2 eggs instead, and you'll be adding more protein to your batter.

**RV Tip**

**Nutrition Tip**

**Cooking Tip**

For those with food allergies: Use barley flour instead of whole wheat flour if you are allergic to wheat, and use soy milk powder if you are allergic to dairy.

# Snacks and Appetizers

Whether you're snacking alone or entertaining the neighbors, these recipes are sure to please! Make a variety of appetizers and throw an RV party!

Snacking can be easy even at the last minute. Use leftovers and get creative. You'll be surprised at the gourmet concoctions you can come up with in a snap. Variations of the old classic cheese and crackers include leftover bread sliced and toasted with various spreads; pear and apple slices topped with cheese; and smoked salmon, trout, or halibut on crackers.

Look for fresh seasonal vegetables at roadside stands to dip into one of your favorite spreads or dips.

# Deviled Eggs

4 hard-boiled eggs
3 tablespoons mayonnaise
1 teaspoon minced garlic
1/2 teaspoon Spike seasoning*
1/4 teaspoon paprika

Remove the shells from the hard-boiled eggs. Slice each egg
in half lengthwise. Remove the yolks and place them in a
small bowl. Add the mayonnaise, garlic, and Spike seasoning to the yolks and mix well. Using a small spoon, fill each
halved egg with the yolk mixture and sprinkle with paprika. Serve immediately or chill for a few hours until ready
to serve.

**Makes 8 deviled egg halves.**

### Variation

For a lower-fat version of this recipe, substitute soy-based
mayonnaise in place of the full-fat variety. You'll get all the
flavor and creaminess of deviled eggs, with a much leaner
fat content.

*Spike seasoning is found in the herb or spice section of most grocery stores. It
is a delicious blend of salt and more than 20 different seasonings.

When the eggs have finished boiling, keep the water for washing dishes. You'll save on hot water bills and conserve energy at the same time.

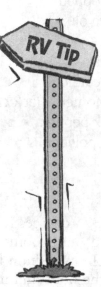

# Mini Quiches

*These little gems are crowd pleasers! Make extra—you can freeze and reheat these for a quick, satisfying treat.*

1 medium onion, minced
6 mushrooms, chopped
1 tablespoon olive oil
1 egg
1/2 cup lowfat milk
1/2 cup whole wheat flour
1 cup shredded Monterey jack cheese
1/2 teaspoon black pepper
1 teaspoon garlic powder
1/4 teaspoon salt
Spray oil

Preheat the oven to 375 degrees F. In a medium frying pan, sauté the onions and mushrooms in olive oil until lightly browned. Set aside. In a medium bowl, whisk the egg and milk together. Add the flour and mix well. Add the cheese, black pepper, garlic powder, and salt. Finally, add the sautéed onions and mushrooms and stir the mixture until well blended. Spray a muffin pan with a generous coating of oil. Spoon the batter into muffin cups, filling each cup half full. Bake for 30 minutes. Remove from the oven and allow to cool for a few minutes. Ease a fork down the sides of each muffin cup to remove each quiche. Serve warm.

**Makes 12 quiches.**

# Crab and Artichoke Dip

1 package (16 ounces) imitation crabmeat
4 ounces lowfat cream cheese, softened
1/2 cup mayonnaise
1/2 cup chopped onion
1 large can (15 ounces) artichoke hearts, drained
   and chopped
3/4 cup grated Parmesan cheese
1 tablespoon garlic powder
Crackers or toasted French Bread

Preheat the oven to 375 degrees F. Mix together the crabmeat, cream cheese, and mayonnaise until well blended.
Add the onion, artichoke hearts, Parmesan, and garlic powder and mix well. Pour the mixture into an 8-inch baking
pan or pie plate and bake for 20 to 25 minutes, until lightly
browned. Serve with crackers or French bread.

**Serves 4.**

# Crabmeat Puffs

*This is a variation of an appetizer that Amy's mom,
Bobbie, loves to prepare when the family is together.
Make lots as they'll go fast in a crowd!*

1/2 cup butter
1 cup shredded sharp Cheddar cheese
1 can (6 ounces) crabmeat, drained
1/2 teaspoon seasoning salt
1/4 teaspoon black pepper
6 English muffins

Preheat the oven to 350 degrees F. In a small saucepan, melt
the butter. Remove from heat and add the Cheddar cheese,
crabmeat, seasoning salt, and black pepper. Split the
muffins in half and place on a baking pan. Spoon the crabmeat mixture onto each muffin half. Bake for 10 minutes,
then broil on low for an additional 3 minutes, until cheese
gets bubbly. Remove from the oven and slice each muffin in
quarters. Serve warm.

**Serves 4 to 6.**

**Variation**

If you don't have English muffins on hand, use slices of
whole grain bread.

# Shrimp Cocktail

1 pound shrimp, shelled
6 cups water
3/4 cup fresh lime juice
1/2 cup chopped onion
1/2 cup ketchup
1/3 cup chopped cilantro
2 tablespoons horseradish
1 tablespoon olive oil
1/4 teaspoon salt

Place the shrimp in a large saucepan with the water and 1/4 cup lime juice. Bring to a boil and cook for 3 minutes. Drain, rinse, and peel the shrimp. Combine the shrimp and remaining 1/2 cup lime juice in a large bowl, cover, and chill for 1 hour. Stir in the remaining ingredients and serve immediately.

**Serves 6.**

Peeled, precooked shrimp are available in most grocery stores and will save you some time. Also, premade cocktail sauce is readily available. Just combine shrimp and cocktail sauce, top with a tablespoon of fresh cilantro, and serve with a slice of lemon or lime.

The lime juice in the water is key, as it gives the shrimp that fresh cool flavor. Bottled lime juice can be used in a pinch.

# Creamy Hummus

*This recipe is from* The What to Eat if You Have Diabetes Cookbook *by Daniella Chace (Contemporary Books, 1999).*

1 can (16 ounces) garbanzo beans, drained
Juice of 2 lemons
1 teaspoon sea salt
1/2 cup water
3 tablespoons flaxseed oil
4 garlic cloves
1/2 cup tahini
1 teaspoon chopped fresh mint
Pita wedges, raw vegetables, or crackers

In a blender or food processor, puree together the garbanzo beans, lemon juice, salt, water, oil, garlic, and tahini until creamy. Stir in the mint and serve with toasted pita wedges, raw vegetables, or crackers. This spread is also delicious on sandwiches.

**Serves 10.**

# Guacamole

*This recipe is from* The What to Eat if You Have Heart Disease Cookbook *by Daniella Chace (Contemporary Books, 2001).*

1 large ripe avocado, minced
2 ripe tomatoes, minced
1 teaspoon garlic powder, or 3 garlic cloves, minced
3 tablespoons fresh lemon juice
1 teaspoon balsamic vinegar
1 scallion, minced
1/4 red onion, minced
Baked corn chips or raw vegetables

Mash all the ingredients together in a serving bowl. Serve with corn chips or vegetables.

**Serves 4.**

If you don't want to spend your time peeling and chopping garlic but do like the flavor fresh garlic imparts, buy a bottle of minced or chopped garlic. You'll find bottled garlic in the produce section of most grocery stores.

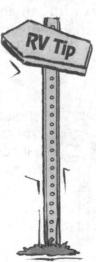

# Cajun French Fries

*This recipe was inspired by Oprah Winfrey's chef Rosie and her Un-Fried Fries from* In the Kitchen with Rosie *(Knopf, 1996).*

4 large baking potatoes
Spray oil, canola, or olive oil
2 egg whites
1 tablespoon Cajun spice
Salt and pepper (optional)

Preheat the oven to 450 degrees F. Slice the potatoes lengthwise into 1/4-inch ovals, and then slice each oval lengthwise into matchsticks. Coat a baking dish with oil. Combine the egg whites and Cajun spice in a sealable plastic bag or bowl and add matchstick potatoes and toss until well coated. Pour the potatoes out onto a baking sheet and spread out in one layer. Bake on the bottom shelf of the oven for 40 to 45 minutes (turning every 6 to 8 minutes) or until fries are golden and crispy. Coat with salt and pepper as desired and serve immediately. Russian Dressing (see page 183) works well as a zesty sauce for these fries.

**Serves 4.**

Nutrition Tip

These fries have very little fat, and the egg whites give this dish protein.

# Cheddar-Pepperoni Melts

1 cup grated sharp Cheddar cheese
2 tablespoons olive spread (tapenade)
15 melba toast crackers, rectangular variety
15 thin slices pepperoni

In a small bowl, combine the grated cheese and olive spread. Arrange the melba toast crackers on an ungreased baking pan. Place a slice of pepperoni on each cracker, then spread cheese and olive mixture on top. Broil on low for 5 to 7 minutes, until cheese has melted. Be careful not to burn these!

**Serves 2 to 4.**

## Variations

Use sliced lunchmeat, smoked salmon, or leftover grilled meat in place of the pepperoni.

# Spicy Garlic Bread

1 can (6 ounces) black olives, pitted
2 tablespoons olive oil
2 teaspoons minced garlic
1 large baguette
1 cup shredded jalapeño jack cheese

Open the can of olives and drain well. Pour the olives into a small bowl. Using the bottom of the can, mash the olives in the bowl until they are broken up into small pieces. Add the olive oil and the garlic and stir well. Slice the baguette in thirds, then slice each third in half, creating 6 pieces of bread. Place the slices on an ungreased cookie sheet. Spread the olive mixture evenly over each slice. Sprinkle cheese over each olive-slathered bread slice. Place in the oven and broil on low for 3 to 5 minutes, checking often to prevent burning. Serve hot from the oven after cheese has melted and begun to bubble.

**Serves 2 to 4.**

## Variation

For crispier bread (this method of cooking produces toasted bread that is chewy in texture), toast the baguette slices for 1 minute on low broil before adding any of the toppings. Once the bread is toasted, add the olive mixture and the cheese and broil for the recommended time.

If you have a baguette that has become too stale to slice, place it in a plastic bag with a lightly dampened paper towel. Seal the bag and allow the bread to sit for a day. You'll find the bread softer and easier to slice once it has regained some moisture.

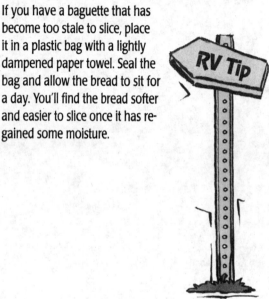

CHAPTER **6**

# A Moveable Feast

## Picnic Lunches

Pack a picnic lunch and go exploring! These quick and easy recipes will fill you up without slowing you down. Enjoy the great outdoors—and a delicious lunch!

Get creative with time-savers such as boxed mixes of tabouli, couscous, hummus, or grain dishes. Most of them just require hot water, and they can be packed in a bowl with a lid for serving on a hike. Pack spicy soy jerky, turkey jerky, or the old standby beef jerky for the ultimate travel food.

A European countryside picnic layout is fun, quick to put together, and a crowd pleaser. Take along your favorite cracker toppers in covered bowls or scalable bags. Then mix and match for fabulous combinations. There's nothing like an array of gourmet delicacies after a hike or a day outside. For example, you can top crusty bread or crackers with pecans, pesto, cheese, tapenade, or smoked salmon. Or if you're indoors and have access to an oven, stack crackers with cheese, then heat them under the broiler for 20 to 30 seconds, just enough to melt the cheese. Scrumptious!

# Roast Beef on Rye

1 teaspoon steak sauce
1 tablespoon mayonnaise
2 slices rye bread
1 teaspoon horseradish
1/4 pound roast beef, thinly sliced
2 slices Muenster cheese
Lettuce for garnish
Tomato for garnish

Combine the steak sauce and mayonnaise and spread on 1 slice of rye bread. Spread the horseradish on a second slice of bread and top with layers of roast beef. Add the Muenster cheese and top with lettuce and tomato. Wrap tightly in aluminum foil or place in a sealable bag. To avoid spoilage, be sure to keep the sandwich cool if you are traveling in hot weather to a picnic site.

**Makes 1 sandwich.**

# Couscous and Vegetables

1 cup water
2 tablespoons olive oil
1 small onion, minced
1 cup chopped broccoli
1 teaspoon Spike seasoning (see Deviled Eggs, page 40,
    for description)*
10 cherry tomatoes, halved
1 cup couscous

Heat the water in a teakettle. Meanwhile, heat 1 tablespoon olive oil in a small saucepan. Add the onion and
broccoli and heat over medium heat for 4 to 5 minutes.
Turn off heat. Add Spike seasoning, tomatoes, and the remaining olive oil. Pour boiling water over the mixture. Add
the couscous and stir well. Cover the saucepan with a lid
and allow it to sit for at least 5 minutes. If you are packing
for a picnic, allow the couscous to chill for 1 hour before
transferring it to a bowl with a lid. While this blending of
couscous and vegetables is perfect on its own, it is also a
wonderful addition to a salad of mixed greens or as a side
dish with smoked salmon, Jarlsberg cheese, and a crusty
baguette.

**Serves 4.**

*If you don't have Spike seasoning, use 1 teaspoon Italian seasoning and
1/4 teaspoon sea salt.

**Variations**

Add any variety of pitted olives to the couscous for additional flavor and texture.

Add a can of chickpeas for a protein boost.

Couscous is so simple to prepare. If you can boil water, you can make couscous! To make a quick side dish, boil 1 cup water, turn off heat, add 1 cup couscous, cover with a lid, and allow to sit for 5 minutes. Serve hot with butter or grated cheese or topped with stir-fried vegetables.

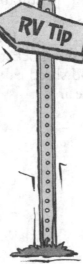

# Curried Tuna Salad

1 can (6 ounces) tuna, in water, drained
1 tablespoon curry powder
1 garlic clove, minced
1 tablespoon fresh lemon juice
1 tablespoon mayonnaise
Dash salt and pepper
Sliced cabbage, spinach, green peppers, or tomatoes
   (optional)

In a small bowl with a lid suitable for picnic travel, combine all the ingredients (except the optional ones). Refrigerate until you are ready to pack for your picnic. Bring along your favorite bread or pita pockets and prepare sandwiches at your picnic site. Add sliced cabbage, spinach, green peppers, or tomatoes, if desired.

**Serves 2.**

# Shrimp Salad

1 can (6 ounces) small shrimp
2 tablespoons mayonnaise
$1/4$ cup finely chopped celery
$1/4$ teaspoon lemon juice
1 teaspoon fresh or dried dill
$1/2$ teaspoon onion powder
Dash salt

In a small bowl with a lid suitable for picnic travel, mix all the ingredients together. Refrigerate until you are ready to pack. Bring a box of your favorite light crackers along—this shrimp salad makes a perfect topping.

**Serves 2 as a light lunch.**

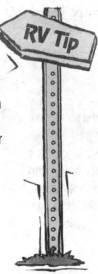

If you really love cooking with fresh herbs, consider growing your own! If you're on the road for an extended trip, you can keep small pots of fresh herbs on your countertop. Place them in the sun during the day when your RV is parked, and simply stow them safely when you're on the move. You'll enjoy their fresh-picked flavor in all your meals.

# Asian Chicken Salad

1 tablespoon mayonnaise
1 tablespoon olive oil
1 teaspoon sesame oil
1 tablespoon soy sauce or tamari
1/4 teaspoon ginger powder
1 tablespoon sesame seeds, plus more for garnish
1 can (10 ounces) white chicken meat
1 head green leaf lettuce
Bok choy
Mung bean sprouts
1 head red cabbage, shredded

In a small bowl with a lid suitable for picnic travel, blend the mayonnaise, olive oil, sesame oil, soy sauce, ginger powder, and sesame seeds. Add the chicken and mix well. Store in the refrigerator until you are ready to pack.

Prepare a salad of lettuce, bok choy, bean sprouts, and cabbage in another storage container. Keep the salads separate until you are ready to eat at your picnic destination. Garnish with sesame seeds.

**Makes 2 large portions.**

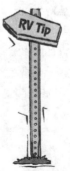

Planning to grill chicken for dinner? Make enough to have leftovers for the next day's lunch. It's a great way to extend the time, effort, and cooking that goes into meal preparation. Enjoy grilled chicken in place of canned in this delicious chicken salad.

# Egg Salad with Roasted Red Peppers

4 hard-boiled eggs, shells removed
2 tablespoons chopped roasted red peppers, drained
1 teaspoon minced garlic, or 2 fresh garlic cloves, minced
1 teaspoon olive oil
1 tablespoon mayonnaise
Dash sea salt
Dash pepper
Italian bread (optional)
Lettuce or sprouts

In a small bowl with a lid suitable for picnic travel, mash the hard-boiled eggs with a fork. Stir in the roasted red peppers, minced garlic, olive oil, mayonnaise, salt, and pepper. Refrigerate until you are ready to pack. To make 2 sandwiches for a picnic lunch, slice 4 pieces of Italian bread. Carry the bread in a sealable bag, and the egg salad, with sprouts or lettuce on top, in a container with a lid. When you are ready for lunch, spread the egg salad on the bread and top with the lettuce or sprouts.

**Serves 2.**

# Smoked Salmon Sandwich

2 teaspoons Dijon mustard
4 pieces whole grain bread
2 tablespoons mayonnaise
1/2 pound smoked salmon
Dash pepper
1 small cucumber, peeled and sliced thinly lengthwise

To make 2 sandwiches, spread 1 teaspoon mustard on each of 2 slices of bread. Spread 1 tablespoon mayonnaise on each of the other 2 slices. Slice the smoked salmon into lengthwise pieces and place on the 2 mustard-coated bread slices. Sprinkle the salmon with a dash of pepper. Place the cucumber slices on top and cover with the remaining mayonnaise-coated bread. Cut the sandwiches in half and place in sealable bags, foil, or a container suitable for picnic travel.

**Makes 2 sandwiches.**

## Variation

Place a slice or two of Swiss cheese on top of the salmon for added taste and texture.

Smoked salmon is a wonderful food to keep on hand. It keeps well in the refrigerator, and because it requires no preparation of its own, it is perfect for a quick, delicious meal or snack. Most grocery stores carry an assortment of flavors ranging from garlic to barbecue.

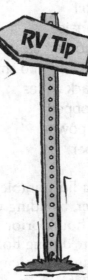

# Italian Tuna Salad

1 can (6 ounces) tuna in water, drained
2 teaspoons olive oil
1 teaspoon mayonnaise
1/4 cup shredded mozzarella
6 fresh basil leaves, torn into small pieces
1/4 cup chopped black olives
1 small tomato, chopped
1/2 teaspoon garlic powder
Dash salt and pepper

In a small bowl with a lid suitable for picnic travel, mix all the ingredients together, blending well. Place in the refrigerator to chill for a few hours prior to your picnic. If you are traveling to a picnic site during hot weather, be sure to keep the tuna chilled. For an easy picnic snack, spread the tuna on your favorite crackers and serve with baby carrots and celery sticks. Or layer the tuna salad with lettuce on slices of whole grain bread or in pita pockets, or roll it up in a flour tortilla.

**Serves 2.**

# Nutty Banana Sandwich

2 slices whole grain bread
1 tablespoon nut butter (peanut, almond, cashew, etc.)
1/2 banana, sliced lengthwise into 4 pieces
1 tablespoon honey
1 tablespoon chopped walnuts

On 1 slice of bread, spread 1 tablespoon nut butter and place banana slices on top. On the other slice of bread, spread 1 tablespoon honey and sprinkle walnuts on top. Put both slices of bread together and cut in half. Enjoy the sweet nutty flavor!

**Makes 1 sandwich.**

You'll find that the layer of oil found at the top of most jars of nut butters can be more easily mixed back in if the jar is stored upside down prior to opening. The oil will naturally rise to the top (which is now the bottom), which will take some of the chore out of blending it yourself.

# Fresh Mozzarella Sandwich

2 pieces bread
2 tablespoons fresh pesto spread
1 ball fresh mozzarella cheese (approximately 2 ounces)
1 large tomato slice
Lettuce for garnish

Toast the bread. Spread 1 tablespoon pesto on each piece of bread. Cut the mozzarella ball into 4 to 6 slices. On 1 piece of bread, arrange the mozzarella slices on top of the pesto. On the other piece of bread, place the large tomato slice on top of the pesto. Add lettuce, put the bread together to form a sandwich, and slice in half.

**Makes 1 sandwich.**

CHAPTER **7**

# Hot Days

## "Cool As a Cucumber" Lunches

On hot days, enjoy the simplicity of these light yet satisfying lunches. Cool off with quick salads and easy sandwiches.

# Spinach Salad

6 cups fresh spinach, washed, with stems removed
4 hard-boiled eggs, shelled and crumbled
1/2 cup chopped walnuts
1/2 cup thinly sliced red onion
1/4 cup raisins
1 can (11 ounces) mandarin orange slices, drained
1/2 cup Parmesan cheese

Combine all the ingredients in a large bowl and toss well. Serve in 4 bowls with your favorite salad dressing, or choose one from chapter 14, "Simply Saucy: Sauces and Dressings."

**Serves 4.**

Look for prewashed spinach in the produce aisle of the grocery store. You won't need to waste any water rinsing and double rinsing your spinach leaves, and you'll save prep time too.

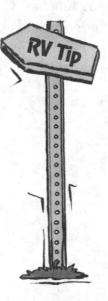

# Tuna and Swiss Roll-Up

2 cans (6 ounces each) albacore tuna in water, drained
2 tablespoons mayonnaise
1 teaspoon minced garlic or 2 fresh garlic cloves, minced
1/2 can (4 ounces) water chestnuts, chopped
1 stalk celery, chopped
Dash salt and pepper
2 large or 4 small flour tortillas
1/2 cup grated Swiss cheese
Mung bean sprouts for garnish

In a small bowl, mix the tuna, mayonnaise, garlic, water chestnuts, celery, salt, and pepper, blending well. Spread mixture evenly on tortillas. Sprinkle Swiss cheese over the tuna and garnish with bean sprouts. Roll the tortilla, tucking in an end to prevent spillage.

**Makes 2 large or 4 small roll-ups.**

# Gazpacho A-Go-Go

*This quickie version of the cool summer classic*
*is refreshing and tangy.*

3 cups peeled and chopped tomatoes
1/2 cup finely chopped onions
1 cucumber, peeled, seeded, and diced
1/2 cup finely chopped peppers (green, red, or yellow)
1/4 cup olive oil
1/3 cup red wine vinegar or balsamic vinegar
2 cups tomato juice
2 garlic cloves, minced
3 tablespoons chopped fresh parsley or cilantro
2 tablespoons chopped fresh chives or dill
1/4 teaspoon cayenne pepper

Put the tomatoes, onions, cucumber, and peppers in a large
bowl or tureen. Whisk the oil, vinegar, and tomato juice together with the garlic, parsley or cilantro, chives or dill, and
cayenne pepper. Pour over the vegetables and toss. Chill for
3 hours or more, covered. Serve cold.

**Serves 4.**

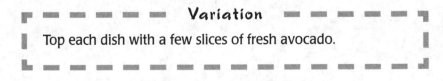

**Variation**

Top each dish with a few slices of fresh avocado.

To help keep lettuce leaves fresh, wrap them in a damp cloth or damp paper towel and place in a plastic bag in the fridge.

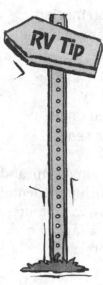

# Lentil Salad with Dijon Cream

1 cup dried lentils
1/2 cup lowfat sour cream
3 tablespoons Dijon mustard
1 tablespoon balsamic vinegar
1/4 teaspoon thyme
1/4 teaspoon black pepper
1 cup chopped celery
3/4 cup chopped red onion
1/4 teaspoon salt or sea salt

Place the lentils in a saucepan and cover with water to 2 inches above lentils. Bring the lentils to a boil; cover, reduce heat, and simmer for 20 minutes, or until tender. Drain well. Move lentils to a large bowl. Add remaining ingredients, toss well, and serve.

**Serves 4.**

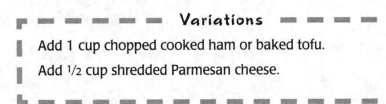

### Variations

Add 1 cup chopped cooked ham or baked tofu.

Add 1/2 cup shredded Parmesan cheese.

Didn't think you wanted to bother cooking beans because they require so much time? Lentils are your answer! Since they only take about 20 minutes on the stove, you can prepare a hearty meal in a short time.

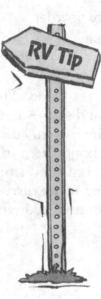

# Curried Pasta Spirals

12 ounces dry pasta spirals, cooked al dente
2/3 cup mayonnaise
3 tablespoons curry powder
1/2 teaspoon sea salt
1 cup red grapes, washed and halved

Drain the pasta and set aside. Mix together the mayonnaise, curry powder, and salt. Add this mixture to the pasta a small amount at a time, evenly distributing the sauce. Add the halved grapes, mixing them in gently. This pasta dish can be made ahead of time and stored in the refrigerator or cooler, as the marrying of textures and flavors in this dish only becomes more pronounced with time.

**Serves 4.**

### Variation

Substitute white flour pasta with whole wheat, or try one of the numerous wheat-free pastas made from quinoa, soy, or rice.

# Smoked Salmon Salad

*The lemon juice, sea salt, and olive oil make
a light, refreshing salad dressing for this
simple and delightful combination.*

2 cups chopped fresh greens
1/2 cup cherry tomatoes
1/3 red onion, sliced paper thin
1 cup crumbled smoked salmon
Juice of 1/2 lemon
1 teaspoon salt or sea salt
2 tablespoons olive oil

Combine all the ingredients in a large bowl and toss well.
Serve immediately.

**Serves 2.**

# BLT with Caesar Dressing

4 slices bread

2 tablespoons Caesar salad dressing (bottled, or see
   page 184)

4 slices bacon, cooked

4 slices fresh tomato

2 leaves romaine lettuce or garden greens (spinach,
   garden mix, etc.)

Toast the bread if desired. Spread Caesar dressing on the
bread and stack with the bacon, tomato, and leafy greens.

**Makes 2 sandwiches.**

Nutrition Tip

For a delicious sandwich
without the meat, substi-
tute vegetarian soy-
based "bacon" strips for
the bacon.

# Asian Noodle Salad

*This recipe was provided by Joanne Brand*
*of Ketchum, Idaho.*
*This cool pasta salad has delicate flavors, a little*
*heat, and real Asian flair. Joanne makes this for*
*her family, and it has become a favorite dish*
*for their weekend camping trips.*

1/2 cup sesame oil
1/2 cup toasted sesame seeds, plus more for sprinkling
1/4 cup tamari or soy sauce
2 tablespoons sugar
2 tablespoons hot chili oil
2 tablespoons balsamic vinegar
1 1/4 pound vermicelli noodles
3 scallions, chopped

Heat water in large saucepan for noodles. Meanwhile, combine the sesame oil, seeds, tamari or soy sauce, sugar, chili oil, and vinegar in a large bowl. Cook the pasta until just al dente, and rinse. Toss the pasta in with the sauce and sprinkle more sesame seeds until well coated. Garnish with scallions and serve at room temperature, or refrigerate and serve later. May be refrigerated for up to 3 days.

**Serves 4.**

# Curried Chicken Salad

*Serve this delicious salad on a bed of mixed greens or use as a topping for rice cakes and crackers.*

1 can (10 ounces) white chicken meat
1/2 cup canned, chopped water chestnuts
2 teaspoons curry powder
1/4 teaspoon cayenne pepper
1 tablespoon mayonnaise
1 small onion, minced
2 mushrooms, finely chopped
Dash salt and pepper

In a small bowl, mix all the ingredients together and serve.

**Serves 2.**

## Variations

Use leftover chicken breasts instead of canned chicken. Simply shred the chicken into small pieces and mix with the remaining ingredients.

Mix in a handful of halved grapes for a fresh, lively flavor addition.

Curry powder is actually a blending of many different spices: cumin, coriander, black mustard seed, fenugreek, and turmeric. For example, by keeping a jar of curry powder in your cupboard, you're actually carrying a whole array of flavors! Use it for spicing up soups, stews, potato dishes, and stir-fry meals.

RV Tip

# Good Sam Club Sandwich

*This is our version of the traditional club sandwich.
Salmon, avocado, and mayonnaise (SAM) is a decadent
combination and especially good on whole grain bread.
Or make up your own club sandwich from your
favorite meats, cheeses, and spreads.*

3 thin slices bread
Condiments such as mayonnaise, mustard, or pesto
Salmon, cold cuts, bacon, or grilled meats
Cheese such as smoked Gouda, sharp Cheddar, or Swiss
Avocado, sprouts, leafy greens, or tomatoes (optional)

Make this layered sandwich by topping the first slice of
bread with condiments such as mayonnaise and mustard,
then some salmon or cold cuts such as ham or turkey, next
another piece of bread topped with cheese(s) and vegetables
(if desired), and finally another slice of bread to finish the
tall sandwich. Slice each sandwich into 4 small squares and
serve.

**Makes 1 large sandwich.**

# Cold Days

---

## Warm and Hearty Lunches

---

Cold days call for the warmth and comfort of hearty, nourishing meals. Curl up with a good book and a hot lunch—and enjoy one of life's simple pleasures.

# Cheesy Bean Quesadillas

4 flour tortillas
1 can refried beans
1 cup grated Monterey jack cheese
Salsa for topping

Place 1 tortilla in a skillet and cover half with 1/4 of the refried beans and 1/4 cup cheese. Heat over medium until the
cheese has melted. Fold tortilla. Repeat with the other
3 tortillas. Serve hot with salsa topping.

**Makes 4 quesadillas.**

Look for instant refried beans the
next time you're shopping for
beans. The instant variety is
easy to store, takes up less
space, and reconstitutes simply
by adding water. You can easily
make just as much as you need!

When using canned re-
fried beans, choose those
that are free of lard,
sodium, sugar, preser-
vatives, or chemicals.
Bearito Brand is our
favorite.

# Smoked Gouda Sandwich with Avocado and Tomato

2 slices whole grain bread
2 slices tomato
2 slices smoked Gouda cheese
1/4 avocado, sliced

Place the bread slices on a broiling pan. Place 1 slice of tomato on each piece of bread, topped by a slice of Gouda cheese. Broil on low for approximately 4 minutes or until cheese is bubbly. Remove from the broiler. Add the avocado slices. Put the bread together to form a sandwich and slice in half. Eat while still warm.

**Makes 1 sandwich.**

# Swedish Crisp Pizza

1 medium onion, chopped
2 tablespoons olive oil
2 tablespoons sun-dried tomato
1 tablespoon minced garlic
2 cups fresh or frozen spinach
1 teaspoon Italian seasoning
Dash salt and pepper
1 Swedish rye crisp round cracker*
1 1/2 cups grated mozzarella cheese

Preheat the oven to 350 degrees F. In a small saucepan, sauté the onion in olive oil until lightly browned. Add the sun-dried tomato, garlic, spinach, Italian seasoning, salt, and pepper until well blended. Turn off heat. Place the rye crisp round on an ungreased cookie sheet. Spread the spinach mixture evenly over the rye crisp round, avoiding the hole in the center. Sprinkle the mozzarella cheese over the top. Bake in the oven for 8 to 10 minutes, until cheese is melted and bubbly. Serve hot out of the oven.

**Makes 1 pizza.**

**Variations**

Replace the spinach with broccoli, mushrooms, or black olives for a taste variation.

Replace the mozzarella cheese with jalapeño jack cheese for a zestier pizza.

*Swedish rye crisps are typically sold in the cracker section of the grocery store. They are packaged in a paper wrapper, usually 6 crisps per package, each approximately 10 inches in diameter.

# Pesto Pasta with Salmon

12 ounces pasta, cooked and drained
1/4 cup pesto
2 cups grilled salmon
1/2 cup grated Parmesan cheese (optional)

Toss the pasta, pesto, and salmon in a large bowl. Sprinkle the top with grated cheese, if desired, and serve.

**Serves 4.**

# Turkey Puff Pies

1 package frozen puff pastry shells (6 per package)
1 small onion, chopped
1 tablespoon butter
$1/2$ cup vegetable broth
5 ounces canned turkey
$1/2$ cup corn, canned or frozen
$1/2$ cup peas, canned or frozen
$1/2$ teaspoon salt
$1/2$ teaspoon pepper
1 teaspoon garlic powder
2 tablespoons nonfat powdered milk
6 slices cheese, any variety

Bake the pastry shells according to the directions on the package. While the shells are baking, sauté the onion in butter until lightly browned. Add the broth, turkey, corn, peas, salt, pepper, garlic powder, and powdered milk and stir well. Heat over medium for 5 minutes. Remove the pastry shells from the oven when finished. Ladle the turkey mixture into each shell and top with a slice of cheese. Put a pastry cap (removed according to the pastry cooking directions) on top of each cheese slice. Bake an additional 10 minutes at 350 degrees F. Serve hot out of the oven.

**Serves 2 to 3.**

Puff pastry shells are incredibly easy to work with. You'll find yourself re-turning to the freezer section of the supermarket again and again once you realize how easy it is to create an impressive, delicious, gourmet meal! Use your imagination and experiment with fillings—you can even give new life to leftovers! Try the Cinnamon Peach Tart (see page 206) for a sweet variation.

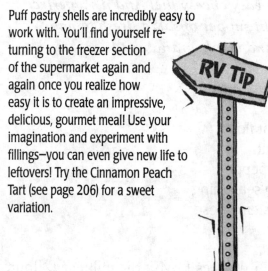

# Grilled Cheese Pie

*Everyone loves this easy cheesy pie! And it's a perfect
addition to a light supper of salad, fresh tomato
slices, and whole grain bread.*

1 cup nonfat or lowfat milk
1 egg, beaten
3/4 cup whole wheat flour
1/4 teaspoon sea salt
1/2 teaspoon black pepper
1/2 teaspoon Italian seasoning
1 cup cubed Muenster cheese
Cooking spray

Preheat the oven to 375 degrees F. Mix the milk, egg, flour,
salt, pepper, and Italian seasoning together. Fold in 1/4 cup
of the cubed cheese. Spray a 9-inch pie pan with cooking
spray. Pour mixture into pan and bake for 20 minutes. Remove from the oven; add the remainder of the cheese to the
top of the pie and bake an additional 10 minutes, until the
cheese on top is melted and bubbly. Serve hot out of the
oven.

**Serves 4.**

**Variations**

Add lightly sautéed broccoli, zucchini, and/or onion to the pie batter.

Use Swiss or Monterey jack cheese as alternatives to Muenster, or combine two different cheeses for a delicious blending of flavors.

This dish is easy to prepare and requires minimal cleanup. Because the pie requires no crust, the preparation time is greatly reduced, allowing for less time in the kitchen and more time in the great outdoors!

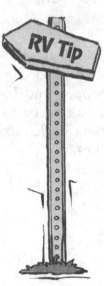

RV Tip

# Spinach-Cheese Soufflé

1 onion, chopped
2 garlic cloves, minced, or 1 teaspoon minced garlic
2 tablespoons olive oil
16 ounces frozen spinach, thawed
1 cup Parmesan cheese
1 cup cubed Swiss cheese
3 eggs
1/2 teaspoon salt or sea salt
1 teaspoon black pepper
2 teaspoons Italian seasoning
Cooking spray

Preheat the oven to 350 degrees F. In a saucepan, sauté the onion and garlic in olive oil for 5 minutes. Add the spinach, cheeses, eggs, salt, pepper, and Italian seasoning and mix well. Spray a 9-inch baking pan or casserole dish with a coating of oil. Pour the soufflé mixture into the baking pan and bake for 40 minutes.

**Serves 2 to 4.**

# Nachos with Chicken and Two Cheeses

1 tablespoon olive oil
1 pound chicken breasts, cut into small pieces
1 tablespoon minced garlic, or 4 to 6 fresh garlic cloves,
    minced
10 to 12 ounces flavored tortilla chips (e.g., cilantro and
    lime, sesame, hot pepper)
Salt
1 1/2 cups grated Swiss cheese
1 1/2 cups grated jalapeño jack cheese

In a large pan, heat the olive oil on medium or high. Add the chicken pieces and garlic and continue to cook for approximately 5 minutes, stirring occasionally. When the chicken is cooked through, turn off heat. In a large baking pan, spread a layer of tortilla chips to cover the bottom. Layer half of the chicken pieces on the chips and sprinkle with salt. Cover the chicken with the Swiss cheese. Spread another layer of chips, following with the remaining chicken, again sprinkling with salt. Cover with the jalapeño cheese. Place the baking pan under the broiler and heat on low for 5 minutes, checking often to prevent burning. Serve while the cheese is still hot and bubbly. Serve the nachos with a bowl of fresh salsa for dipping. If you like a hot and spicy flavor, top the nachos with our Mexican Hot Sauce (see page 182).

**Serves 4.**

# Pepperoni Pizza

Frozen pizza dough
Pasta sauce or barbecue sauce

## Baked Topping Ideas
Pepperoni
Vegetarian pepperoni alternative
Cheese, such as sharp Cheddar, mozzarella, smoked
   Gouda, pepper jack
Artichoke hearts
Sun-dried tomatoes
Roasted chicken (or other leftover grilled meat)
Pine nuts

## After-Baking Topping Ideas
Fresh tomatoes
Greek olives

Start with ready-made pizza dough, found in the freezer section of the grocery store, and follow the package directions for baking. Spread a layer of pasta sauce or barbecue sauce over the pizza, and add your favorite toppings for baking. Bake for 20 minutes at 350 degrees F, or until the cheese is hot and bubbly. Add tomatoes or olives; slice and serve.

**Makes 1 pizza.**

**Variations**

Add basil, garlic, or cheese directly to the soft pizza dough and knead them in before baking for a gourmet flair.

If you can't find frozen pizza dough, the easiest choice is the prebaked Italian bread Boboli, which is available in the large family pizza size or individual pizza size.

If you like a spicy sauce, add garlic powder, onion powder, and/or fresh ground pepper directly to the sauce.

If you are still at home preparing for a weekend trip, you have the option of making dough before you leave and freezing it. Make enough for several pizzas ahead of time and freeze for later use.

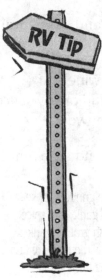

# Easy Marinated Burgers

1 pound lean ground beef
Balsamic Vinegar Marinade (follows) or Garlic Marinade
(follows)

Form 4 patties out of the beef and marinate in one of the
following marinades for 5 minutes. Grill or fry in a skillet,
flipping once, until thoroughly cooked.

**Serves 4.**

### Balsamic Vinegar Marinade
2 tablespoons balsamic vinegar
2 tablespoons tamari or soy sauce

Combine ingredients and store until ready to use.

### Garlic Marinade
2 tablespoons red wine
2 tablespoons tamari or soy sauce
1 teaspoon garlic powder

Combine ingredients and store until ready to use.

You can now buy spice grinders for sea
salt, dried onion, dried garlic, and spice
combinations. The fresh ground garlic
adds true garlic flavor without all the fuss
of chopping or pressing fresh garlic.

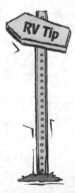

# CHAPTER 9

# Sensational Sides

Add variety to your main meals with these delicious side dishes. For a lighter meal, pair one or two with a salad and a slice of hearty bread.

# Baked Beans

*This recipe is from* The What to Eat if You Have
Heart Disease Cookbook *by Daniella Chace
(Contemporary Books, 1999).*

1 tablespoon extra virgin olive oil
1/2 yellow onion, chopped
3 garlic cloves, chopped
2 cups cooked adzuki, kidney, or pinto beans
1 tablespoon molasses
1 tablespoon tamari or soy sauce
1 teaspoon dry mustard

Preheat the oven to 350 degrees F. Heat the olive oil in a
large ovensafe skillet. Add the onion and garlic and sauté
over medium heat until the onion is translucent. Add the
beans, molasses, tamari, and mustard. Stir well. Place the
skillet in the oven and bake for 20 minutes, or until golden
brown.

**Serves 4.**

# Parmesan Polenta

3 cups water
2 cups nonfat or lowfat milk
1 1/2 cups dry polenta
1 teaspoon sea salt
1/4 teaspoon black pepper
1/2 cup Parmesan cheese
2 tablespoons butter

In a large saucepan, bring the water and milk to a boil. Add the polenta, reduce heat, and stir. Heat on very low for 8 minutes, stirring occasionally. Add the salt, pepper, Parmesan, and butter and stir well. Continue to heat for 2 more minutes. Remove from heat and serve immediately.

**Serves 4.**

# Ginger-Curry Carrots

1 pound baby carrots
1/2 cup orange juice
1 teaspoon garlic powder
2 tablespoons sugar
2 tablespoons butter
1/4 teaspoon ginger powder
1/2 teaspoon curry powder

Combine all the ingredients in a medium saucepan and bring to a boil. Reduce heat to low, cover, and cook an additional 6 to 8 minutes. Serve hot, using remaining liquid as a sauce for topping.

**Serves 4.**

Baby carrots are a great food to keep on hand for snacking, picnic lunches, and side dishes. Ready to eat right out of the bag, they require no rinsing or peeling, saving water and prep time.

Use fresh fruits and vegetables when available, and save canned and frozen foods as backups.

# Baked Herbed Fries

1 large russet potato
1 sweet potato
1 tablespoon extra virgin olive oil
1/4 teaspoon crushed rosemary
1/4 teaspoon crushed basil
1/2 teaspoon paprika
1 teaspoon sea salt

Preheat the oven to 450 degrees F. Slice the potatoes into long thin strips. In a large bowl, combine the potatoes with the remaining ingredients. Toss until the potatoes are well coated with oil and herbs. Spread onto a baking sheet. Bake for 15 minutes. Remove from the oven and turn the potatoes over. Bake an additional 15 minutes, or until golden brown.

**Serves 2.**

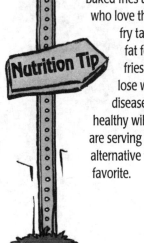

Baked fries are perfect for those who love that satisfying French fry taste without all the fat found in traditional fries. Those who want to lose weight, avoid heart disease, or generally stay healthy will appreciate that you are serving them a healthy alternative to an American favorite.

# Gary's String Beans and Shrimp

10 large shrimp, peeled
2 cups green string beans
1 tablespoon olive oil
1/2 tablespoon tamari

Sauté the shrimp and green beans in a pan with the olive oil, tossing occasionally. Sprinkle the top with tamari and serve as soon as the shrimp are well cooked (opaque). Be careful not to overcook the shrimp, as they will get tough.

**Serves 2.**

# Broccoli with Garlic and Parmesan

2 tablespoons olive oil
1 tablespoon minced garlic, or 6 fresh garlic cloves,
  minced
3 cups chopped broccoli
1 tablespoon tamari
$1/2$ cup water
Parmesan cheese

In a large saucepan, heat the olive oil and garlic for 1 minute. Add the broccoli. Mix the tamari and water together and pour over the broccoli. Heat on low, covered, for 5 minutes. Remove from heat and serve immediately, topping each serving with a generous amount of Parmesan cheese.

**Serves 2 to 4.**

The RV lifestyle often takes us far from grocery stores and roadside stands where fresh produce is readily available. For adventures into remote deserts and mountains, keep a supply of canned and frozen vegetables on hand. You'll welcome the convenience of opening a can or reaching into the freezer when you're preparing your meals far, far away from the hustle and bustle of the world!

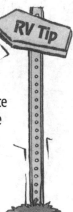

# Cheese and Garlic Stuffed Potatoes

4 baking potatoes
1 tablespoon butter or olive oil
2 teaspoons minced garlic, or 4 fresh garlic cloves, minced
1/2 cup nonfat or lowfat milk
1/2 cup sharp Cheddar cheese
1 tablespoon chopped parsley
2 teaspoons thyme
1/4 teaspoon sea salt or table salt
1/4 teaspoon black pepper

Pierce the potatoes with a fork and bake at 350 degrees F
for 1 hour. Remove from the oven. Split open each potato
and scoop out the pulp, leaving a shell 1/4 inch thick. Re-
serve the shells and set aside the potato pulp in a bowl.
Heat the butter or olive oil in a skillet over medium heat.
Add the garlic and sauté for 30 seconds. Add the milk and
bring to a simmer. Pour the milk mixture over the potato
pulp and mix in 1/4 cup of the cheese and the parsley, thyme,
salt, and pepper. Stuff the shells with the potato mixture.
Sprinkle evenly with the remaining 1/4 cup cheese and bake
at 500 degrees for 8 minutes, or until the cheese begins to
brown.

**Serves 4.**

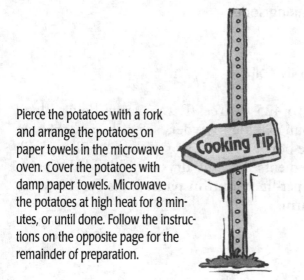

Pierce the potatoes with a fork and arrange the potatoes on paper towels in the microwave oven. Cover the potatoes with damp paper towels. Microwave the potatoes at high heat for 8 minutes, or until done. Follow the instructions on the opposite page for the remainder of preparation.

# Cornbread

1 1/2 cups cornmeal
1/2 cup unbleached wheat flour
2 teaspoons baking powder
1/2 teaspoon sea salt
1/2 teaspoon baking soda
1 egg
1 cup milk
3 tablespoons olive oil

Preheat the oven to 425 degrees F. In a large bowl, blend the cornmeal, flour, baking powder, sea salt, and baking soda. In a separate bowl, beat the egg with the milk and oil. Mix the wet ingredients into the dry until blended. Spoon the batter into paper-lined muffin pans. Bake for 15 to 20 minutes. Serve warm.

**Makes 8 muffins.**

### Variation

Add 1/2 cup well-drained corn for added texture and fiber.

# Citrus Beets

2 large beets, scrubbed and sliced
1 tablespoon butter
1 tablespoon grated orange rind
2 teaspoons lemon juice
1/4 teaspoon salt
1/8 teaspoon black pepper
1/4 cup slivered almonds

Place the beets in a large saucepan, cover with water, and bring to a boil. Cover with a lid, reduce heat, and simmer for 10 minutes, or until al dente. Drain off the water and add the butter, orange rind, lemon juice, salt, and pepper and bring to a simmer, stirring occasionally for a few minutes, until the sauce cooks down to a glaze. Top with almonds and serve hot.

**Serves 6.**

# Nutty Rice Pilaf

*This rice dish is tasty on its own and exceptional with curry. Try the Sweet Potato Curry (see page 130) with it for a superb combination. The rice is colorful and festive, perfect for entertaining.*

2 tablespoons olive oil
3-inch piece of cinnamon stick
1/2 teaspoon freshly ground black pepper
1 1/2 cups basmati rice
3/4 teaspoon sea salt
2 cups water
2 tablespoons golden raisins
1/4 cup roasted cashews
1/4 cup sliced pistachios

Heat the oil, cinnamon stick, and pepper in a skillet over medium heat for 2 minutes, until fragrant. Add the rice and salt and stir well to coat with oil. Add the water and bring to a boil. Reduce heat and cook covered over low heat for 15 minutes without removing the lid. Then remove from heat and stir in the raisins, cover the pot with a clean dish towel, and set aside for 5 minutes. Stir in the nuts and serve hot.

**Serves 4.**

---

### Variation

Add 5 cardamom pods, 5 whole cloves, or ¼ teaspoon saffron threads to the rice before adding water.

---

Some grocery stores and many natural food stores now offer bulk food sections in which an array of dried fruit, nuts, grains, and mixes is available. These items are typically lower in price than their prepackaged counter-parts found on the shelves. Additionally, you can purchase just the amount you want, so there's less waste.

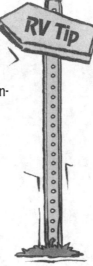

# CHAPTER 10

# Gourmet Grilling

Cooking in the great outdoors seems to make everything taste better! Enjoy your "outdoor kitchen"—you may find yourself cooking dinner on the grill every night!

## Tips for Grilling

As grilling methods vary considerably, it is best for you to use your own judgment with regard to cooking times. We have given you the cooking times that worked well for us as we tested these recipes on a gas grill. You will be successful in preparing these recipes if you keep an eye on the grill and the food!

Aluminum foil is an excellent tool for preparing grilled vegetables. It is easy to use, requires no cleanup, and is recyclable. Think of the foil as a minicasserole dish. The food is prepared and sealed inside, concentrating the heat for efficient cooking. The natural juices and flavors of foods are locked in, resulting in moist, perfectly cooked meals.

## CORN IN FOIL

Husk and remove the silk threads from ears of corn, leaving a few husks in place. Spread butter over the kernels and sprinkle with salt or your favorite seasoning. Place the husks over the kernels and wrap each ear in foil. Place on the grill for at least 20 minutes, turning a few times during the cooking process.

## MIXED VEGETABLES IN FOIL

Chop zucchini, onions, tomatoes, and peppers into small pieces and place in a bowl. Sprinkle olive oil and seasoning over the vegetables and mix well. Place the vegetables on a large sheet of foil. Fold the foil around the vegetables and tightly seal the edges. Cook on a hot grill for 10 minutes, turning the foil pouch a few times for even cooking.

## POTATOES IN FOIL

To speed the cooking process, cut potatoes into small pieces. Mix in a bowl with olive oil or butter and a sprinkling of salt and pepper. Place each sliced potato in its own sheet of heavy-duty foil (or 2 layers of regular foil) and wrap tightly, sealing the edges to prevent moisture loss. Place on the grill or over hot coals and cook for at least 30 to 45 minutes, checking for doneness before serving.

## GRILLING BURGERS

Buy lean ground beef that is from organically fed cattle when possible. Add seasonings to the hamburger meat and mix in well before forming patties for the grill. Some of our favorite seasonings are fresh or powdered garlic, cayenne, sea salt, pepper, paprika, chili powder, dried onion, or cumin. Shredded Parmesan cheese can be mixed into the meat, or try our Mexican Hot Sauce (see page 182) for a Southwest flair. Baste your burgers with barbecue sauce, or a little tamari for a change, and top your burgers with Russian Dressing (page 183), Simple Caesar Dressing (page 184), or Avocado Dressing (page 181) for a real treat.

## GRILLING BREAD

Cut thick slices of Italian bread and coat with a light layer of olive oil. Place the bread on a hot grill and cook until toasted, flipping once.

# Katie's Garlic Flank Steak

2 pounds flank steak
Marinade (follows)

Place the flank steak in the Marinade and allow it to soak for at least 1 hour. Cook on a hot grill for approximately 7 minutes per side. Test for doneness before removing the steak from the grill. When the steak is finished cooking, allow it to sit for 5 minutes, then slice the steak into thin pieces diagonally.

### Marinade
1/3 cup tamari
2 tablespoons balsamic vinegar
2 tablespoons olive oil
3 to 5 garlic cloves, minced

In a nonmetal pan, whisk together all ingredients. Set aside until ready to use.

**Serves 4.**

If you want to get one step ahead in your food preparation, you can prepare many of your marinades and meats before your trip and simply freeze them for later grilling. Prepare the marinade as directed and pour it into a sealable bag. Add the meat or fish, toss the bag a few times, and place the bag in the freezer. Thaw before grilling.

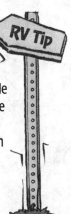

# Scotch Salmon

1 pound salmon cut into 2 pieces (or use 2 steaks)
Marinade (follows)

Rinse the salmon and pat it dry with a paper towel. Place the salmon in the Marinade and allow it to marinate for 1 to 2 hours. When ready to cook, place the salmon on a hot grill, saving the Marinade for basting. Cook approximately 10 minutes, basting once or twice during cooking. Remove from the grill and serve hot.

### Marinade
2 tablespoons Scotch Whiskey
2 tablespoons lemon juice
1 teaspoon Italian seasoning
Dash salt and pepper

In a medium-sized bowl suitable for marinating, mix the marinade ingredients together. Set aside until ready to use.

**Serves 2.**

# Satay Skewers with Asian Dipping Sauce

## Skewers

*Choose your favorites from the following meats or vegetables.*

Chicken breast (cut into 2-inch cubes)
Beef steak (cut into 2-inch cubes)
Fish such as salmon (cut into 2-inch cubes)
Eggplant
Mushrooms
Cherry tomatoes
Red, yellow, or green bell peppers (chopped into 2-inch pieces)
Sweet onions (chopped into 2-inch pieces)

Alternate the chunks of meat and vegetables on bamboo or metal skewers. To keep them from sticking to the grill, spray the pieces with olive oil before grilling. Remember to turn them as they brown. Cooking time will vary depending on the food.

## Asian Dipping Sauce

*Recipe by Lynn McCarthy of Cottonwood Catering and Cooking School in Ketchum, Idaho.*

1/4 cup tamari or soy sauce
1/2 cup oyster sauce
1/2 cup white wine
1 scallion, diced

1 tablespoon brown sugar
1/4 cup water
1 tablespoon minced fresh ginger
Dash pepper

Place the tamari or soy sauce and oyster sauce in a bowl and whisk together. Slowly add the wine and continue whisking. Stir in the remaining ingredients. Refrigerate for at least 1/2 hour for the flavors to meld. Use just enough of the sauce to coat the meat and vegetables, and allow them to marinate for 1/2 to 1 hour prior to grilling. Place extra sauce in a small bowl and use it as a dipping sauce for the grilled meats and vegetables.

**Makes 1 1/4 cups of marinade or dipping sauce.**

Punch holes in a plastic bag and use it for storing mushrooms in the refrigerator. They'll keep longer this way.

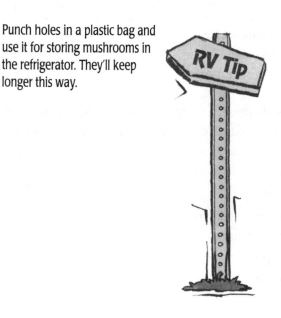

# Tempting Tuna with Mustard Butter

1 pound tuna steaks (cut into 2 pieces)
Marinade (follows)
Mustard Butter (follows)

Rinse the tuna steaks and pat them dry with a paper towel. Place the tuna in the Marinade and spoon the Marinade over the top. Allow the tuna to soak in the Marinade for at least 1 hour. Meanwhile, prepare the Mustard Butter topping. When the tuna has finished marinating, place it on a hot grill and cook approximately 10 minutes, turning once during cooking. Serve hot off the grill with a generous topping of Mustard Butter.

### Marinade
1 tablespoon mayonnaise
2 tablespoons olive oil
1 tablespoon Dijon mustard

In a shallow pan suitable for marinating, mix together all ingredients to make marinade. Set aside until ready to use.

### Mustard Butter
2 tablespoons butter
1 tablespoon Dijon mustard
1 tablespoon mayonnaise
1/4 cup chopped parsley
2 scallions, minced

In a small saucepan, melt the butter. Mix in the remaining ingredients and heat over low for 2 minutes. Set aside until ready to use.

**Serves 2.**

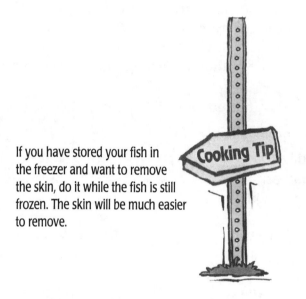

If you have stored your fish in the freezer and want to remove the skin, do it while the fish is still frozen. The skin will be much easier to remove.

# Maui Mahi Mahi

1 pound Mahi Mahi fillet
Marinade (follows)

Rinse the fish and pat it dry with a paper towel. Cut the fish into approximately 16 large chunks and place them in a medium bowl suitable for marinating. Pour the Marinade over the fish. Allow the fish to marinate for an hour. When ready to grill, thread the fish on skewers and cook over a hot grill approximately 8 minutes, turning once. Serve hot off the grill.

### Marinade
2 tablespoons butter
1 tablespoon olive oil
1 tablespoon tamari
1 tablespoon lemon juice
1 teaspoon sugar
1 teaspoon minced garlic, or 2 fresh garlic cloves, minced
1/4 teaspoon black pepper

Melt the butter in a small saucepan. Add remaining ingredients and stir well. Set aside until ready to use.

**Serves 2.**

If you are using wooden skewers, be sure to soak them in water for at least 30 minutes prior to grilling, as they may burn if they are too dry.

# Terrific Turkey Burgers

1 egg
1 pound ground turkey
3/4 cup seasoned bread crumbs or stuffing mix
1 teaspoon onion powder
1 teaspoon garlic powder
1 teaspoon tamari
1/4 teaspoon black pepper
Rolls, buns, or bread
Condiments or vegetables (optional)

In a medium-size bowl, beat the egg and mix in the turkey, bread crumbs or stuffing mix, onion and garlic powder, tamari, and pepper. Form into 4 patties, making a hole in the center of each patty.* Cook over a hot grill approximately 4 minutes per side. Remove from the grill and serve on bread of your choice.

Top turkey burgers with your favorite condiments, or spread salsa, Guacamole (page 47), or Creamy Hummus (page 46) on top and layer with sprouts, lettuce, and fresh tomato. Or add a slice of cheese on each burger just before taking them off the grill.

**Makes 4 burgers.**

*The hole in the center of each burger will assist in even cooking.

---

**Variations**

For spicier burgers, add a dash of cayenne pepper or Tabasco sauce to the mix.

For a light cheese flavor, add 1/2 cup Parmesan cheese.

---

**Nutrition Tip**

Buy free-range chicken for a higher-quality meat.

# Eastside Grilled Chicken

1 pound skinless chicken breasts
Marinade (follows)

Prepare Marinade. Rinse the chicken and pierce its surface with a fork. Place the chicken in the bowl with the Marinade and allow it to marinate for 1 to 2 hours. Cook on a hot grill for approximately 10 minutes, turning once during cooking time. Serve hot off the grill.

### Marinade
2 tablespoons olive oil
2 tablespoons tamari
$1/2$ cup water
$1/4$ teaspoon black pepper
Pinch of cayenne powder or chili powder

Mix all ingredients and set aside until ready to use.

**Serves 2.**

# Grilled Eggplant Sandwich

*Inspired by our local organic bakery,*
*Bigwood Bakery in Ketchum, Idaho.*

1 medium eggplant
Olive oil
2 tablespoons pesto
4 slices bread, or 2 fresh rolls
4 tablespoons blue cheese
4 tablespoons roasted red peppers

Peel the eggplant and slice into pieces 1/4 to 1/2 inch thick. Pour a little olive oil onto a plate and coat both sides of each eggplant slice with oil. Place on a hot grill and cook for 5 minutes on each side. Remove the eggplant from the grill and set aside to cool. Spread pesto on the bread and layer with eggplant, blue cheese, and roasted red peppers.

**Makes 2 sandwiches.**

# Zesty Marinated Shrimp

32 large shrimp (approximately 1 to 1¼ pounds), shelled,
   deveined, and rinsed
Marinade (follows)

Add the shrimp to the marinade and stir well. Allow the
shrimp to marinate for at least ½ hour in the refrigerator.
To grill, place 4 to 6 shrimp on each skewer. Save the Marinade and set aside. Arrange the skewered shrimp on the
grill over hot coals. Cook approximately 6 to 8 minutes,
turning once during cooking and basting with the remaining Marinade. Remove the shrimp from the skewers and
serve hot. Serve the grilled shrimp with rice or pasta, or toss
the grilled shrimp with a mixed green salad.

### Marinade
¼ cup olive oil
2 tablespoons lemon or orange juice
1 tablespoon tamari
1 tablespoon garlic powder
1 teaspoon salt
1 teaspoon pepper
1 cup water

Mix all ingredients in a bowl or saucepan with a lid. Set
aside until ready to use.

**Serves 4.**

## Variation

Use this same recipe for stovetop cooking. If you were planning to grill outdoors but find the weather has not cooperated, simply cook the shrimp in the saucepan in which it was marinating. After marinating for 1/2 hour, place the saucepan with the shrimp on the stove, stir once, and then cover with a lid. Heat over low for approximately 4 minutes, stirring a few times during cooking. The shrimp are ready when they have turned bright pink. Remove the shrimp from the stove. Serve over rice, using the remaining cooked marinade as a sauce along with the shrimp.

Shrimp are a great source of protein, and the leftovers are delicious as a cold appetizer.

If you are using wooden skewers for grilling, be sure to soak them in water for at least 30 minutes prior to grilling to prevent burning.

# Mid-Western Sparerib Rub

*Lynn McCarthy of Cottonwood Catering and Cooking School in Ketchum, Idaho, shared this recipe, revealing her secret to perfect grilling: "It's in the rub." The main ingredients of this recipe come from the "rub," which combines a variety of spices and flavors.*

2 tablespoons sea salt
2 tablespoons mild or hot paprika
1 1/2 tablespoons ground cumin
1 tablespoon oregano
3/4 teaspoon ground cinnamon
2 teaspoons onion powder
1 1/2 teaspoons garlic powder
1 teaspoon black pepper
1/4 teaspoon allspice

Mix all the ingredients together and rub lightly onto meat.* Place the meat in a large sealable bag and refrigerate for at least 2 hours but not more than 10. Cook the meat over a hot grill until thoroughly cooked (time will vary depending on meat).

**Makes enough rub for up to 6 pounds of meat.**

*Apply the above directions for the rub to your meat of choice (spareribs, chicken breasts, pork tenderloin).

Prepare this rub recipe prior to your trip and store it in a tightly sealed jar. It will keep for up to 6 months in the freezer. Double or triple the recipe depending on your needs.

**RV Tip**

**Nutrition Tip**

This rub does not add any fat to the meat, creating a more healthful meal. Additionally, each spice has its own unique health benefits; for example, garlic is a natural antibiotic and cinnamon helps stabilize blood sugar levels.

# CHAPTER 11

# Pressure Cooker and One-Pot Meals

Enjoy the hearty dishes in this chapter after a day of adventuring. You'll love the ease of preparation—and the results!

# Sweet Potato Curry

1/2 onion, chopped
3 tablespoons red curry paste (Patok's brand or other)
1 tablespoon olive oil
2 cups chopped sweet potato
Any vegetables of choice (optional)
Any meat of choice (optional)
2 cups chicken broth
1 can (14 ounces) reduced-fat coconut milk
1/4 cup chopped cilantro leaves*
Steamed rice, cooked greens, or steamed vegetables

Sauté the onion with the curry paste in oil over medium heat for 2 minutes. Add the sweet potato and any other vegetables or meat desired and cook for 2 minutes. Add the broth and coconut milk and reduce heat to low.** Simmer for 12 minutes. Sprinkle the top with cilantro and serve over rice, greens, or vegetables.

**Serves 4.**

#### Variation

Add chopped eggplant, garlic, or other vegetables to the potatoes to vary this dish.

*Cilantro is also known as coriander leaves, not to be mistaken for Italian parsley.

**Do not boil the coconut milk, as it will separate.

# Quick Chicken Chowder

1 medium onion, chopped
1 tablespoon minced garlic
2 tablespoons olive oil
2 cups chicken broth
1 pound chicken breasts, cut into 1-inch cubes
2 teaspoons thyme or herb of choice
1 cup fresh, frozen, or canned corn
1 cup fresh, frozen, or canned peas
1 can (15 ounces) whole white potatoes, drained, cut into
   thirds
1/2 cup flour
Salt and pepper to taste

In a large saucepan, sauté the onion and garlic in olive oil until lightly browned. Add the chicken broth. Add the chicken cubes and cook over high heat until the broth begins to boil. Reduce heat to medium. Add herbs, corn, peas, and potatoes and cover with a lid. Heat over medium for 8 minutes, then sprinkle the flour over the mixture and stir well. Heat an additional 1 minute on medium. Ladle from the pot into bowls, adding salt and pepper as desired. Serve hot.

**Serves 4.**

# Pot Roast with Onions and Root Vegetables

*If you like the ease of pressure cooking hearty meat dishes, you'll love* Pressure Cooking the Easy Way *by Maureen Keane and Daniella Chace (Prima Publishing, 1997). This is a sample recipe from that book.*

3 pounds roast (chuck, loin, round, sirloin), trimmed of visible fat
2 to 4 tablespoons barbecue rub (or spice of your choice)
Cooking spray
2 onions, sliced into thick rings
1 cup burgundy wine
1 cup nonfat chicken broth
1 cup water
3 large carrots, chopped
2 medium potatoes, peeled and chopped
2 medium sweet potatoes, peeled and chopped
2 medium turnips, peeled and chopped

Coat meat with barbecue rub. Spray the pressure cooker with cooking spray and brown the roast and half of the onions. Add the wine, broth, and water. Cover and bring to high pressure and cook for 50 minutes. Cool quickly by placing the pot under cold water. Open and add the rest of the onions and the remaining ingredients. Replace the lid and bring to high pressure again and cook for 10 minutes. Cool quickly and serve.

**Serves 6.**

Nutrition Tip

Carrots are loaded with healthy carotenoids that protect our eyes and improve our vision.

# Gary's Hearty Beef Stew

*Think of this recipe as a template that can be altered.*
*For example, if you love garlic, you could use 20 cloves;*
*if you like pepper, use more than is called for; or feel*
*free to omit any of the recipe's ingredients you don't*
*happen to have handy or you don't particularly like.*
*This recipe is very adaptable.*

1/4 cup organic canola or olive oil
1 small to medium beef roast
2 teaspoons sea salt
1 tablespoon black pepper
2 large onions, chopped
4 to 7 garlic cloves, coarsely chopped
4 cups chicken, beef, or vegetable broth
4 medium potatoes, chopped

Heat the oil in an open pressure cooker over high heat. Slice the roast into several slabs. Rub both sides thoroughly with salt and pepper. Thoroughly brown both sides of the meat in the oil over medium-high heat (this takes about 5 minutes). Then remove the meat and set aside to free up the pan for sautéing the onions. Add water and chopped onions and garlic to the pan and bring back up to medium-high heat, stirring the onions and garlic to caramelize them evenly. Add the broth and potatoes. Lock the pressure cooker lid into place and bring up to high pressure for about 5 minutes, then reduce to low heat for about 30 minutes.

**Serves 4 to 6.**

**Nutrition Tip**

Buy organic free-range beef for a healthy meat with the best flavor.

# Simple Fish Stew

1 medium onion, chopped
1 tablespoon olive oil
3 cups water
1 pound codfish, cut into 2-inch cubes
1 cup chopped celery
2 cups sliced carrots (1/4-inch pieces)
1 can (15 ounces) sliced potatoes
2 tablespoons butter
1 tablespoon garlic powder
1/2 teaspoon salt
1/2 teaspoon pepper
1 cup nonfat milk powder
Parmesan cheese (optional)

In a large saucepan, sauté the onion in olive oil until lightly browned. Add the water, fish, celery, carrots, potatoes, butter, garlic powder, salt, pepper, and milk powder. Cover with a lid and heat on low to medium for 15 minutes. Ladle the stew into bowls and serve hot. Sprinkle Parmesan cheese over each serving for a simple yet delicious topping.

**Serves 4.**

Nonfat milk powder can enhance many dishes. It adds creaminess without adding fat and is easy to use and store. Keep a box handy, or even better, store your powdered milk in a sealable bag or small container for more efficient use of your limited pantry space.

Fish is rich in essential fatty acids, which are healthy fats that make our skin soft and act as an anti-inflammatory helping to relieve arthritis.

# Lentil and Coriander Soup

1 cup dried lentils, rinsed
2 cups water
1 large carrot, cut julienne style
1 large yellow onion, chopped
1 stalk celery, finely chopped
2 to 4 garlic cloves, crushed, or 1 to 2 teaspoons minced
   garlic
2 tablespoons extra virgin olive oil
1 can (14 ounces) peeled crushed tomatoes
4 teaspoons ground cumin
1/2 teaspoon coriander
1/2 teaspoon sea salt
2 tablespoons balsamic vinegar
Parmesan cheese and black pepper (optional)
Whole grain bread

Cook the lentils in the water for 20 minutes in a large saucepan. Sauté the carrot, onion, celery, and garlic in olive oil for 10 minutes in a skillet. Add the sautéed vegetables and the tomatoes, cumin, coriander, salt, and balsamic vinegar to the cooked lentils. Cook an additional 10 minutes on low heat. Ladle the stew into bowls and top with coarsely grated Parmesan cheese and a dash of black pepper. Serve with hearty slices of bread.

**Serves 4.**

To eliminate the need for two separate cooking pots (skillet and saucepan), use the saucepan to prepare the sautéed vegetables first, then set the vegetables aside in one of the serving bowls while the lentils cook. You'll save yourself the extra cleanup time and use less of your RV's water supply.

Lentils are loaded with fiber, something we all need more of in our diets.

# Creamy Potato Soup

5 medium potatoes, chopped
2 cups chopped onion
2 large garlic cloves, minced, or 1 heaping tablespoon
   minced garlic
3 tablespoons olive oil
4 cups water
1 cup nonfat milk powder
2 cups potato flakes
1 teaspoon salt
1 teaspoon black pepper

In a large pot, cook the potatoes in enough water to cover. Remove from heat and drain when the potatoes are still firm, about 15 minutes. Place the potatoes in a bowl and set aside. Using the same large saucepan, sauté the onion and garlic in 1 tablespoon olive oil. Add the remaining 2 tablespoons olive oil and the remaining ingredients, stirring well. Add the cooked potatoes, and heat over medium heat for 10 to 15 minutes.

**Serves 4.**

---

**Variations**

Top with grated Parmesan cheese.

Crumble 4 hard-boiled eggs over the finished soup for added protein and flavor.

Sauté carrots along with the onion and garlic.

# Harvest Soup

1 medium onion, coarsely chopped
3 garlic cloves, minced
2 tablespoons olive oil
1 medium butternut squash, peeled, seeds removed, cut
    into large chunks
2 cups vegetable broth
1/4 teaspoon black pepper
1/2 teaspoon sea salt
1 teaspoon Spike (or other multiseasoning of choice)
Parmesan cheese (optional)
Bread of choice

Using a pressure cooker without the lid, sauté the onion and garlic in olive oil until lightly browned. Add the squash, broth, pepper, salt, and Spike or other seasoning and stir well. Place the lid on the pressure cooker and seal shut. Over medium heat, bring the pressure cooker up to pressure. Continue cooking on medium for 10 minutes. After 10 minutes, turn off heat and allow pressure to be released. Stir well. Serve the soup hot with a generous topping of Parmesan cheese and a slice or two of hearty bread.

**Serves 2.**

# Chunky Vegetable Chili

*This recipe is an adaptation of Chunky Vegetable Chili from* Pressure Cooking the Meatless Way *by Maureen Keane and Daniella Chace (Prima Publishing, 1996). It's great served with a slice of crusty bread.*

2 tablespoons extra virgin olive oil
5 large mushrooms, sliced
1 zucchini, chopped
1 carrot, chopped
1 yellow onion, sliced
3 garlic cloves, minced, or 1 1/2 teaspoons minced garlic
3 cups vegetable broth
1 cup kidney beans, presoaked
1 can (28 ounces) plum tomatoes with juice, halved
1 teaspoon tamari or soy sauce
2 tablespoons chili powder
1 can (8 ounces) tomato paste

Heat the olive oil in an open pressure cooker over medium heat. Sauté the mushrooms, zucchini, carrot, onion, and garlic for 5 minutes. Add the broth, kidney beans, tomatoes, tamari, and chili powder. Seal the cooker and bring to high pressure slowly. Lower heat and cook for 15 minutes. Reduce pressure quickly under cold running water. Add the tomato paste and stir.

**Serves 4.**

r — — — — — **Variations** — — — — — ┐

Add chopped yellow bell pepper for additional color and flavor.

Add cubes of beef for a heartier meal.

L — — — — — — — — — — — — — — — ┘

# Sherry Chicken with Garlic

*This recipe is from* Pressure Cooking the Easy Way
*by Maureen Keane and Daniella Chace
(Prima Publishing, 1997). This dish is excellent
served with red wine and a fresh salad.*

4 halved chicken breasts
4 medium potatoes
1 cup dry sherry
6 garlic cloves, minced, or 3 teaspoons minced garlic
10 cherry tomatoes, halved
1/2 cup chopped Italian parsley

Combine the chicken, potatoes, sherry, and garlic in a pressure cooker. Seal and heat under high pressure for 10 minutes. Quickly reduce pressure. Top the chicken with halved
cherry tomatoes and chopped Italian parsley.

**Serves 4.**

If you have a small amount of wine left in
the bottle, don't toss it. Fill ice cube
trays with the remaining wine and
place in the freezer. After the cubes of
wine have frozen, remove them from the
ice cube trays and store them in the freezer
in a sealable bag or other small container.
When you need just a small amount of wine
for a recipe, you'll have it ready to pop out of
the freezer!

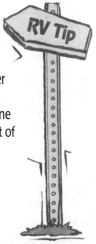

# CHAPTER 12

# Sumptuous Suppers

## Everyday Comfort Meals

Dinner on the road needn't be boring! In this chapter, you'll discover an array of delicious recipes suited to every palate.

# Joni's Meat Loaf

3 tablespoons chopped onion (more if desired)
Dash salt and pepper
2 tablespoons Worcestershire sauce
1 teaspoon dry mustard (or hot mustard)
1 egg
3/4 cup milk
1 cup bread crumbs*
1 1/2 pounds lean ground beef
1 teaspoon ground dried onion and/or garlic, dried
   oregano, or parsley
Fresh chopped celery (optional)

Preheat the oven to 350 degrees F. Mix together the onion, salt and pepper, Worcestershire sauce, dry mustard, egg, and milk. Blend well, then add the bread crumbs and ground beef. Add herbs and celery. Place the mixture in a loaf pan and bake for 1 hour. Slice leftovers for delicious meat loaf sandwiches the next day.

**Serves 6.**

*If you don't have bread crumbs, make your own by finely chopping a few slices of old bread.

## Variations

Make this recipe into meatballs simply by omitting the milk. Roll the meat mixture into small balls and fry in a small amount of oil to brown. Then drain the oil and bake in 1 can of mushroom soup and a dollop of sour cream. Serve with rice or steamed vegetables. Or, bake in a pan with spaghetti sauce for another easy meatball variation.

# Beef Stroganoff

1 tablespoon butter
1 pound beef sirloin, cut into 1/4-inch-wide strips
2 garlic cloves, minced
1/2 teaspoon sea salt
1/4 teaspoon black pepper
2 cups mushrooms, thinly sliced
1/2 cup chopped onion
1 cup cold water
1 tablespoon Worcestershire sauce
1/2 cup lowfat sour cream
1 package wide egg noodles, cooked and drained
1 teaspoon ground dried onion and 1 teaspoon ground
   dried garlic (optional)

Heat the butter in a large skillet over medium heat. Add the
beef and garlic and sauté for 1 minute. Season with salt and
pepper, then add the mushrooms and onions and continue
cooking for 2 minutes. Add the water and bring to a boil,
then reduce heat to a simmer. Continue to simmer for about
15 minutes, until mushrooms are soft, then add Worcestershire sauce and sour cream. Heat an additional 2 minutes.
Serve over wide egg noodles. Sprinkle with dried onion and
garlic powder, if desired.

**Serves 4.**

# Turkey with Rice

1 cup basmati rice
2 cups water
1 tablespoon tamari or soy sauce
1 pound boneless, skinless turkey breast, cut into 2-inch
  chunks
2 cups chopped carrots
1/2 cup chopped celery
1 teaspoon garlic powder
Dash salt and pepper

Preheat the oven to 400 degrees F. In a large baking pan with a lid (or aluminum foil in place of the lid), mix the rice, water, and tamari or soy sauce. Add the remaining ingredients and mix well. Cover with the lid or foil and bake in the oven for 40 minutes, until the rice has absorbed the liquid and is completely cooked. Serve hot from the oven.

**Serves 2 to 4.**

Turkey and chicken are inter-
changeable in many recipes.

Cooking Tip

# Fish Burritos with Corn Salsa and Cilantro

1 cup canned corn
1 cup fresh salsa, medium to hot
$1/4$ teaspoon cumin
$1/2$ teaspoon onion powder
$1/2$ teaspoon garlic powder
$1/2$ teaspoon salt
1 cup fresh cilantro
4 large whole wheat tortillas
1 pound salmon or other fish, baked and cut into small pieces
1 cup shredded jalapeño Monterey jack cheese

Preheat the oven to 350 degrees F. In a medium-sized bowl, combine the corn, salsa, spices, salt, and cilantro. In a large baking pan, place 1 tortilla, opened flat. Layer the tortilla with a quarter of all the ingredients: salmon, corn-salsa mixture, shredded cheese. Roll the tortilla around the ingredients tightly and push toward the edge of the pan to make room for the remaining 3 tortillas. Continue filling each tortilla until all 4 are filled and arranged side by side in the pan. Bake for 30 minutes. Serve hot.

**Makes 4 burritos.**

**Variations**

Use leftovers from the night before as a substitute for the baked fish. This will save you time and energy.

Make enchiladas by covering the tortillas with 1 can enchilada sauce just prior to baking.

Add broccoli, zucchini, or mushrooms to the filling.

Bake the fish in foil for easy cleanup. You can use the foil as a prep area for cutting up the fish after it's been baked.

**RV Tip**

**Nutrition Tip**

Corn and salsa are both lowfat and a fun way to eat your vegetables.

# Parmesan Noodles

8 ounces uncooked spaghetti
1 cup minced onions
1 teaspoon minced garlic
1 tablespoon olive oil
1/4 cup lowfat sour cream
1/2 teaspoon salt
1/4 teaspoon black pepper
1/3 cup grated Parmesan cheese

Cook the pasta according to package directions. Drain the pasta and set aside. In a large skillet over medium heat, sauté the onion and garlic in olive oil for 4 minutes. Add the cooked pasta and the sour cream, salt, and pepper. Stir well and serve with a sprinkle of Parmesan on top of each serving.

**Serves 4.**

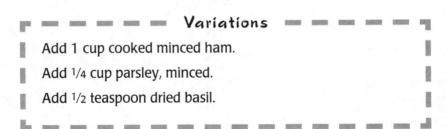

**Variations**

Add 1 cup cooked minced ham.

Add 1/4 cup parsley, minced.

Add 1/2 teaspoon dried basil.

Nutrition Tip

Buying lowfat sour cream saves you loads of calories and tastes just the same to most people.

# Hearty Meat Sauce with Pasta

1 large onion, chopped
3 garlic cloves, minced, or 1½ teaspoons minced garlic
3 tablespoons olive oil
Chopped broccoli, diced green peppers, or sliced
   mushrooms (optional)
12 ounces lean ground beef
1 or 2 jars (28 ounces) tomato sauce
1 can (6 ounces) black olives
¼ teaspoon sea salt
½ teaspoon pepper
1 teaspoon Italian seasoning
12 ounces any variety pasta, cooked and drained
Parmesan cheese

Sauté the onion and garlic in a saucepan in 2 tablespoons
olive oil until lightly browned. Add chopped broccoli, diced
green peppers, or sliced mushrooms for a healthy flavor
boost (optional). Add the ground beef and cook for 2 minutes. Stir in the tomato sauce, black olives, salt, pepper, and
Italian seasoning. Cook over low heat for 10 minutes,
adding 1 additional tablespoon olive oil at the end of cooking to bring out the flavors. Serve the sauce over the cooked
pasta and top with Parmesan cheese.

**Serves 6.**

Prechop onions and store them in the freezer in an airtight container. Simply remove what you need for each recipe and store the rest for another meal.

Use a meat alternative in place of the beef, such as the soy-based Veggie Ground Round. It's delicious and reduces the cholesterol and saturated fat in this dish.

# Crunchy Baked Fish

Cooking spray
1 medium onion, chopped
6 garlic cloves, minced (about 1 tablespoon)
1 1/2 cups seasoned stuffing
2 fillets of white firm fish of your choice
Dash salt and pepper
1 cup vegetable broth

Preheat the oven to 400 degrees F. Coat a small pan with cooking spray and sauté the onion and garlic until lightly browned. Set aside. Coat a broiler-safe baking pan or pie pan with cooking spray. Sprinkle 1 cup seasoned stuffing on the bottom of the pan. Place the fish fillets on top of the stuffing. Spread the sautéed onion and garlic over the fillets. Sprinkle with a dash of salt and pepper. Cover the fillets with the remaining (1/2 cup) stuffing. Gently pour the vegetable broth over the fish and stuffing. Bake uncovered for 30 minutes. To make the topping extra crispy, broil on low for 5 minutes. (Cooking time may need to be increased depending on the type and thickness of fish fillets. Always test the center of fish for doneness.)

**Serves 2.**

Use any fish fillets that hold together well when baked, and vary the spices to fit your tastes.

# Irish Steak

1 red onion, sliced thin
1/2 head of red cabbage, sliced thin
2 tablespoons extra virgin olive oil
1 pound beef sirloin, cut into 1/4-inch-wide strips
2 tablespoons balsamic vinegar
1/4 cup horseradish (optional)

Sauté the onion and cabbage in oil over medium-high heat for about 5 minutes, or until they begin to soften. Add steak strips and continue cooking until meat is cooked and begins to brown. Splash with balsamic vinegar and serve hot. Horseradish can be served on the side or as a topping for this dish.

**Serves 4.**

# Garlic Salmon in Foil

*This fantastic recipe was inspired by Dean and Wendy
Hagin. The use of foil in this recipe produces a moist,
tender, melt-in-your-mouth dish with a rich garlic flavor.*

1 pound salmon fillet, rinsed
1 tablespoon olive oil
3 garlic cloves, thinly sliced
1/4 teaspoon sea salt
1/2 teaspoon freshly ground pepper
1 teaspoon dried dill, thyme, or rosemary (optional)

Preheat the oven to 350 degrees F. Lay the fish on a large
sheet of foil. Rub the fillet with olive oil and evenly distribute the garlic slices over the surface of the fish. Sprinkle the
fish with salt, pepper, and an herb of your choice. Seal the
foil tightly around the fish and place it in a shallow baking
pan. Bake for 40 minutes. To be sure the salmon is ade-
quately cooked, open the foil carefully and insert a knife
into the fillet at the thickest part. The salmon should be
flaky and opaque.

**Serves 4.**

The use of foil in this recipe makes cleanup quick and easy. Simply discard (or recycle, if possible) the foil!

Fish oil contains omega-3 fatty acids, which reduce blood pressure in those with moderate hypertension. Studies have shown that by adding 2 servings of fish to your diet per week you will reduce your risk of a future heart attack by 50 percent.

# Halibut in Puff Pastry

1 medium onion, minced
2 tablespoons butter
1 pound halibut fillet, cut into 2-inch cubes
2 garlic cloves, minced (about 1 teaspoon)
1 cup peas
1 cup thinly sliced baby carrots
1 can (15 ounces) sliced potatoes, drained
1/2 cup water or vegetable broth
1/2 teaspoon salt
1/2 teaspoon pepper
1 teaspoon ground rosemary or other herb of choice
Cooking spray
1 sheet puff pastry dough, thawed*

Preheat the oven to 400 degrees F. In a large saucepan, sauté the onion in butter until lightly browned. Turn off heat. Add the fish, garlic, peas, carrots, potatoes, broth, salt, pepper, and herbs and stir well. Spray the bottom of a baking pan or pie pan with cooking spray. Pour the ingredients from the saucepan into the baking pan. Unfold a puff pastry sheet and place over the top of the baking pan, tucking the edges in around the pan. Bake for 30 minutes, until pastry has become light brown and flaky. Serve hot out of the oven.

**Serves 2 to 4.**

*Puff pastry sheets come packaged in different ways. For this recipe, choose the variety that is sold 2 sheets per box. It is easy to use and requires no preparation time, other than thawing. Store the remaining sheet in the freezer for later use.

## Variation

If you're running low on fresh vegetables, use a can of your favorite soup in place of vegetables and water in this recipe. Your fish pie will take on the flavorings in the soup, creating a delicious meal with minimal prep time.

# Scallops in Lemon Butter

1 pound large bay scallops
3 tablespoons butter
1 tablespoon olive oil
1 tablespoon lemon juice
Dash black pepper
Linguine, cooked and drained

Rinse the scallops and set aside. In a medium saucepan, heat the butter and olive oil until the butter has melted. Add the lemon juice and pepper. Add the scallops and stir well. Heat over medium for just a few minutes, stirring to distribute the sauce. Test a scallop for doneness: the center should be opaque. Serve over linguine, using the remaining lemon butter as a topping.

**Serves 4.**

When you are along the coast, take advantage of the wonderful fresh seafood. You can purchase seafood that has just been caught that day and enjoy it for dinner that night. It doesn't get much fresher than that!

RV Tip

Nutrition Tip

Use extra virgin organic olive oil when possible, as it is one of the healthiest oils for cooking and using in uncooked sauces. "Extra virgin" denotes the very first pressing of the olives, therefore no chemicals are needed to extract the oil. The word "organic" means that no chemical herbicides or pesticides were used on the olive trees and that the olives have not been genetically engineered.

# CHAPTER 13

# The Adventurous Feast

## Ethnic Cooking Made Easy

Take a trip around the world as you enjoy the rich flavors and zesty seasonings of these meals. Your taste buds will enjoy the journey!

When eating out, take note of any special seasonings and flavors in the ethnic food and ask chefs for their specialties. Incorporate these flavors and foods into your own cooking. Keep an eye out for specialty grocery stores and markets, roadside stands with prepared local delicacies, and so on. Expand your palate and open your mind to the possibilities of new flavors while you support the local economy.

# Greek Salad

1 cucumber, peeled and thinly sliced
1 cup cherry tomatoes, halved
1/4 red onion, thinly sliced
1/2 cup feta cheese, crumbled
2 tablespoons olive oil
2 tablespoons balsamic vinegar
1 tablespoon fresh lemon juice
8 Greek olives, pitted and halved

Toss all the ingredients together in a large bowl and serve immediately, or store in a covered container in the fridge for up to 3 days. The flavors meld and the vegetables marinate and the salad is delicious days later.

**Serves 4 to 6.**

When you only need a portion of a whole onion, use the end with the growing tip and store the root end, which will keep much longer.

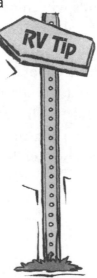

# Jeff's Cajun Fish

1 pound catfish or trout (2 pieces)
Cajun blackened seasoning*
1 tablespoon butter
1 tablespoon olive oil
Lemon wedges

Rinse the fish and pat dry. Generously sprinkle blackened seasoning over the entire skinless side of the fish. In a large skillet or saucepan, heat the butter and olive oil. When the butter has melted, place the fish skin-side-up in butter-oil mixture. Cook on medium for 5 minutes, turning the pan often to distribute the butter, oil, and seasoning. After 5 minutes, check the fish for doneness. Thicker fish may require additional cooking. Serve hot with a squeeze of lemon juice.

**Serves 2.**

*You'll find a variety of seasoning blends in the spice section of the grocery store. If you want the zestiness of Cajun cooking, choose a seasoning blend with a high proportion of red pepper. Amy likes to use a variety called Cajun's Choice Blackened Seasoning, which has a delicious, tangy flavor.

# Borscht

3 cups shredded cabbage
4 cups organic vegetable broth
2 cans (15 ounces) shoestring beets with liquid
1 teaspoon tamari or soy sauce
2 tablespoons balsamic vinegar
1 teaspoon honey

Cook the cabbage and broth in a saucepan over medium-high heat for 10 minutes. Then add the remaining ingredients and continue to cook for 5 minutes. Serve hot or cold.

**Serves 10.**

### Variations

Use fresh beets if available.

Use beef, chicken, or vegetable broth in this soup to vary the flavor. Beef is the traditional stock used in this Russian recipe.

Many grocery stores now carry a variety of broth and soups in 32-ounce aseptic boxes. These boxed soups store easily and need no refrigeration until they are opened. As this recipe calls for 4 cups of broth, you'd simply use an entire box.

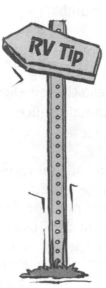

# Eggplant Parmesan

1 medium eggplant (approximately 1 pound)
1 egg
1/2 cup flour
1 cup dried bread crumbs
Cooking spray
1 teaspoon garlic powder
1 teaspoon Italian seasoning
1/2 pound mozzarella cheese, sliced
1 jar (26 ounces) tomato sauce
1 cup Parmesan cheese

Wash the eggplant and slice into pieces 1/2 inch thick. Beat the egg in a bowl large enough to accommodate the eggplant slices. On a large plate or flat surface, pour the flour onto one area and bread crumbs onto another. One-by-one, dip both sides of each eggplant slice first into the flour, then into the egg, then finally into the bread crumbs.

Coat a large broilerproof baking pan with cooking spray. Place each eggplant slice into the pan. Once all the slices are in the baking pan, coat them with cooking spray. Place the baking pan in the oven broiler on high for 3 to 5 minutes. Remove the baking pan from the oven, flip each eggplant slice over, coat with spray oil, and return to the oven for 3 to 5 more minutes on high broil. Eggplant slices should be crispy and browned.

Remove from the oven. Preheat the oven to 400 degrees F. Sprinkle garlic powder and Italian seasoning over each eggplant piece, then top with a slice of mozzarella. Follow this with the tomato sauce, which should be spread thickly to cover all the eggplant. Top with Parmesan. Cover with foil and bake for 10 minutes, then remove foil and bake an additional 15 minutes. Check the eggplant for doneness (it should cut easily and have lost its firmness).

**Serves 4.**

Make the most of your preparation time and RV's fuel supply by preparing more than you might consume in one sitting. Leftovers are a great way to extend your meal. This dish is wonderful the next day either heated up or as a delicious sandwich filling.

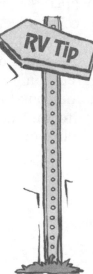

# Spanish Rice

1 medium onion, chopped

4 tablespoons olive oil

1 small red bell pepper, chopped

1 teaspoon minced garlic, or 2 garlic cloves, minced

1 teaspoon cumin

1 teaspoon paprika

1 teaspoon cayenne pepper

1/2 teaspoon salt

1 teaspoon black pepper

2 cups basmati rice, cooked

Sauté the onion in 3 tablespoons olive oil until translucent. Add the bell pepper, garlic, cumin, paprika, cayenne pepper, salt, and black pepper and cook for 2 minutes over medium heat. Add the mixture to the cooked rice, adding the remaining tablespoon of olive oil at the end of preparations. Stir well and serve hot.

**Serves 2.**

Prepare twice as much rice as you need for this recipe and freeze the rest. You'll be using your RV's fuel supply efficiently, as well as cutting down on prep time for a future meal. Store the rice in a sealable bag in the freezer and use it later for stir-fries, side dishes, or soups.

# Chinese Chicken with Cashews

2 tablespoons olive oil
1 cup thinly sliced carrots
2 cups chopped broccoli
1 pound boneless, skinless chicken breast, sliced into thin
strips
1 cup water
2 tablespoons tamari or soy sauce
1 tablespoon sesame oil
1 tablespoon garlic powder
1/4 cup chopped cilantro (optional)
1 cup roasted, salted cashews
Toasted sesame seeds (optional)

In a large skillet or saucepan, heat the olive oil. Add the carrots and broccoli and cook over medium for 2 minutes. Add the chicken and stir well. In a cup or bowl, combine the water, tamari or soy sauce, and sesame oil and pour over the chicken and vegetables. Add the garlic powder and stir well. Cover with a lid and heat over medium for 5 minutes, stirring occasionally. If desired, add cilantro to the mixture in the last minute of cooking. Add the cashews just prior to serving. Serve over rice. Top with sesame seeds for extra texture and flavor.

**Serves 2.**

# Thai Noodles with Shrimp and Red Curry

1 medium onion, chopped
2 tablespoons olive oil
1 tablespoon minced garlic, or 6 garlic cloves, minced
1 small red pepper, chopped
2 cups chopped broccoli
2 teaspoons tamari or soy sauce
1/2 tablespoon red curry paste*
1 can (14 ounces) lowfat coconut milk
1/2 teaspoon salt or sea salt
1 pound raw shrimp, deveined and shelled
1 package (16 ounces) rice noodles, cooked according to
    package directions and drained
1 slice lemon or lime

In a large cook pot, sauté the onion in olive oil until lightly
browned. Mix in the garlic, red pepper, broccoli, and
tamari or soy sauce. Cook over medium heat for 3 minutes.
In a cup or small bowl, stir the red curry paste into a small
amount of coconut milk, blending well. Add the remainder
of the coconut milk, salt, and the coconut-curry mixture to
the vegetables. Stir well. Add the shrimp and cook over
medium heat for 5 minutes, or until the shrimp turn pink.
Serve over rice noodles. Squeeze lemon or lime over the
dish for flavor enhancement.

**Serves 4.**

*You'll find red curry paste in the ethnic section of most grocery stores.

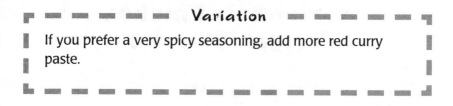

**Variation**

If you prefer a very spicy seasoning, add more red curry paste.

Prepare the rice noodles ahead of time and set aside in a colander. Use the same pot to prepare the shrimp and vegetables, simply adding the rice noodles to the mixture at the end of cooking. One less pot to clean!

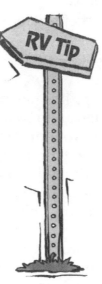

# Vivienne's Chicken Teriyaki Burritos

1 pound boneless, skinless chicken breast, cut into small
  strips
Teriyaki marinade sauce (or use tamari sauce)
1 cup rice
1 tablespoon olive oil
1 can (15 ounces) black beans
4 (12-inch) flour tortillas
2 small tomatoes, chopped (or substitute with 1/2 cup
  fresh salsa)
1/2 cup grated cheese

Place the chicken strips in a nonmetal container. Pour just
enough marinade or tamari to completely coat the chicken. If
you use a lidded bowl, you can "toss" the chicken to ensure
good coverage. Let the chicken marinate for 30 minutes.
Meanwhile, cook the rice, using a larger saucepan than necessary to make mixing easy later on. When the chicken has
finished marinating, heat the olive oil in a large saucepan or
skillet. Add the chicken, including the marinade sauce, and
heat on medium for approximately 8 to 10 minutes, until the
chicken is cooked through. When the rice has finished cooking, add the chicken and the can of black beans to the pot
and stir well. Warm the tortillas in the skillet you just used
for the chicken. Place 1/4 of the rice-bean-chicken mixture in
the middle of each tortilla, leaving room around the edge.
Add tomatoes (or salsa), cheese, and any other condiment
you like. Chopped lettuce or salad mix, chopped onion, and
black olives are tasty additions. Fold, eat, and enjoy!

**Makes 4 burritos.**

# Swedish Meatballs

1 pound ground beef
3/4 cup dry bread crumbs
1/4 cup chopped onion
1 egg, lightly beaten
1 teaspoon sea salt
1/4 teaspoon black pepper
1 1/2 tablespoons Worcestershire sauce
1 cup milk
2 tablespoons butter
2 tablespoons flour
1 cup light cream

In a large mixing bowl, combine the beef, bread crumbs, onion, egg, salt, pepper, Worcestershire sauce, and 3/4 cup milk. Blend well. Shape the mixture into approximately 36 small balls. Heat the butter in a large skillet and brown the meatballs a few at a time, setting them aside on paper towels when done. When all the meatballs have been browned, add the flour to the skillet and stir to mix with meat juices. Cook for one minute, then add the remaining 1/4 cup milk and the light cream. Stir well, then add the meatballs. Cover and simmer for 10 minutes.

**Serves 4.**

# Dean's Shrimp-Fried Rice

1 cup rice
3 tablespoons olive oil
2 eggs, lightly beaten
2 garlic cloves, minced, or 1 teaspoon minced garlic
1 cup chopped broccoli
1 cup julienne-style carrots
1 cup minced onion
1 pound shrimp, peeled, deveined, and rinsed
1 tablespoon tamari or soy sauce
1 tablespoon Szechwan stir-fry sauce (optional)

Cook rice and set aside. In a large skillet, heat 1 tablespoon of oil over medium heat. Add the eggs and cook until just done, allowing them to form a thin, flat omelet. Remove from skillet and cut into thin 1-inch strips. Pour the remaining 2 tablespoons of oil into the skillet, add the garlic, and cook for 1 minute over medium heat. Add the broccoli, carrots, and onion and cook for approximately 3 minutes. Add the shrimp and continue to cook until the shrimp turn pink. Add the tamari, Szechwan sauce, cooked eggs, and rice, blending the mixture well. Heat over high for another few minutes until the rice is hot. Remove from heat and serve immediately.

**Serves 2 to 4.**

### Variation

Replace or supplement any of the vegetables in this recipe with the following: bok choy, green peas, red cabbage, or zucchini.

# CHAPTER 14

# Simply Saucy

## Sauces and Dressings

Enhance the flavor and variety of your meals with luscious sauces and dressings. You'll wake up your taste buds!

# Lemon-Herb Marinade

*Use this delicately seasoned marinade for grilling vegetables such as zucchini, red bell peppers, and mushrooms.*

2/3 cup olive oil
1/3 cup fresh lemon juice
1/3 cup dry vermouth
2 tablespoons dried rosemary, crumbled
1 tablespoon dried thyme, crumbled
1/2 teaspoon sugar
1/2 teaspoon sea salt
1/2 teaspoon black pepper

Whisk all the ingredients in a bowl to blend. This marinade can be made up to 2 days ahead of time and kept covered in the refrigerator. Bring to room temperature before using.

**Makes 1 1/3 cups.**

# BBQ Sauce

*Recipe by Lynn McCarthy of Cottonwood Catering*
*and Cooking School in Ketchum, Idaho.*

2 tablespoons butter
1/2 cup minced celery
3 tablespoons minced onion
1 cup ketchup
3 tablespoons fresh lemon juice
2 tablespoons brown sugar
2 tablespoons cider vinegar or white vinegar
1 tablespoon Worcestershire sauce
1 teaspoon dry mustard
Dash black pepper

In a small saucepan, melt the butter and sauté the celery
and onion until soft, about 6 minutes. Add the ketchup,
lemon juice, brown sugar, vinegar, Worcestershire sauce,
and mustard and season to taste with pepper. Bring to a
boil. Turn the heat down and simmer for 15 minutes. Remove from heat and cool. Baste on ribs and other cuts of
meat during last part of grilling, then serve cooked meat
with sauce on the side or as a topping. Store extra sauce in
the refrigerator.

**Makes 2 cups.**

# Peppy Peanut Sauce

1 cup minced onion
1 tablespoon olive oil
1/2 teaspoon cayenne pepper
1 teaspoon garlic powder
1 1/2 cups vegetable broth
1 tablespoon lemon juice
1 cup natural peanut butter

Sauté the onion in olive oil until lightly browned. Add remaining ingredients and stir well to blend. Continue to heat over low for 3 minutes, stirring constantly. Remove from heat and use immediately as a warm sauce over pasta, rice, or vegetables.

**Makes about 3 cups.**

Instead of squeezing fresh lemons each time you need lemon juice, buy a bottle of 100 percent lemon juice, found in the frozen fruit juice section of the supermarket. It keeps for months in the refrigerator, and it saves time and extra cleanup. When you do use fresh lemons (or any citrus fruit), store the rinds in the freezer for future use as zest in recipes. No more running out to the store for one lemon!

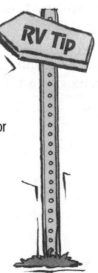

# Avocado Dressing

1 ripe avocado, mashed
1/2 cup plain yogurt
1 teaspoon tamari
1/2 teaspoon garlic powder
2 tablespoons olive oil

Mix all the ingredients in a small bowl or blender until creamy. Use immediately as a salad dressing or spread for sandwiches.

**Makes enough for 2 servings.**

# Mexican Hot Sauce

1 tablespoon minced onion
1 garlic clove, minced
3 tablespoons olive oil
1 tablespoon chili powder

Sauté the onion and garlic in oil for 3 minutes. Add the chili powder and simmer for 5 to 10 minutes. Use this spicy sauce to top bean dishes, chili rellenos, enchiladas, burritos, tostadas, and eggs.

**Makes enough for 4 servings.**

## Variations

Add ⅛ teaspoon cayenne pepper for a hotter version of this sauce.

Add 1 tablespoon semisweet chocolate chips at the very end of the cooking time to make this a molé sauce.

Add 1 tablespoon lemon or lime juice to give this a fresh citrus flavor.

# Russian Dressing

1/3 cup mayonnaise
2/3 cup plain nonfat yogurt
1/2 cup tomato juice
1 tablespoon tamari or soy sauce
1/2 teaspoon hot pepper sauce (Tabasco)
Squeeze of fresh lemon

Combine all the ingredients and mix until smooth.

**Makes enough for 6 to 8 servings.**

Nutrition Tip

This dressing is lower in fat than the traditional recipe, but using lowfat mayonnaise can make it even lower. It is zesty, creamy, sweet, sour, and salty. It makes a great French fry dip, meat sauce, burger topping, and salad dressing.

# Simple Caesar Dressing

3 tablespoons extra virgin olive oil
Juice of 1 lemon
1/2 teaspoon sea salt or table salt
4 garlic cloves, minced
1/4 cup Parmesan cheese

Combine all ingredients in a large bowl. Toss 2 cups washed and chopped greens in Simple Caesar for a quick tangy salad. This dressing can also be used on sandwiches such as the BLT with Caesar Dressing (see page 76).

**Makes enough for 2 servings.**

To get the most juice from a lemon, drop it in hot water for a few minutes, then squeeze.

# Simple Enchilada Sauce

1 can (14.5 ounces) chopped tomatoes
2 tablespoons chopped sweet onion
1 medium jalapeño pepper, chopped
4 garlic cloves, minced
1 teaspoon ground cumin
1 teaspoon dried oregano
1 cup vegetable broth

Process all the ingredients in a blender for 3 minutes, or until well blended. Add an additional ½ cup broth if necessary for the sauce to be smooth. Makes 2 cups.

**Makes enough for 4 servings.**

If you don't have a blender, you can make a chunky version of this sauce by combining all the ingredients in a bowl.

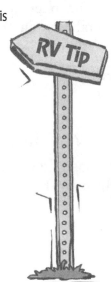

# Ginger Dressing

*This recipe is from* The What to Eat if You
Have Diabetes Cookbook *by Daniella Chace
(Contemporary Books, 1999).*

1/2 orange
1 (2-inch piece) fresh gingerroot, peeled
5 garlic cloves
2 tablespoons tamari
2 tablespoons balsamic vinegar
1 tablespoon extra virgin olive oil or flaxseed oil

Peel the orange by cutting off just the outside bright orange part of the peel, leaving the inner white pithy part, which contains all of its beneficial bioflavonoids. Combine all the ingredients in a blender and blend for 30 seconds to 1 minute. If you prefer a creamier dressing, blend longer. To thin the dressing, add a tablespoon of water and blend again. Serve over leafy greens or mixed dark green vegetables.

**Makes enough for 4 servings.**

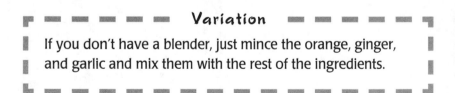

**Variation**

If you don't have a blender, just mince the orange, ginger, and garlic and mix them with the rest of the ingredients.

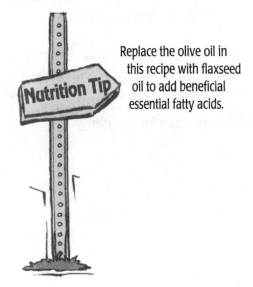

Replace the olive oil in this recipe with flaxseed oil to add beneficial essential fatty acids.

# Sweet Mustard Sauce

*This recipe is from* The What to Eat if You Have Heart Disease Cookbook *by Daniella Chace (Contemporary Books, 2001).*

1/2 cup crushed pineapple, canned or fresh
2 tablespoons hot mustard

Cook the pineapple and mustard in a small saucepan over medium heat for approximately 4 minutes. Use as a dipping sauce for chicken, fish, or other seafood.

**Makes enough for 4 servings.**

# CHAPTER 15

# Temptations for Travelers

## Easy Desserts and Treats

 You'll satisfy your sweet tooth with these decadent treats. They're so easy to prepare, you'll find yourself making dessert every night!

### Dessert Tips

*   Love ice cream sandwiches? Make them yourself using shortbread or chocolate-coated biscuits with your choice of ice cream. Sandwich the ice cream between cookies and refreeze for 5 to 10 minutes, until firm.

*   For a quick party, whip together toppings for ice cream: warm stewed pears or apples, candied ginger, chocolate chips, honey, coconut, fresh fruit, or cookie crumbles.

- Make your own ice pops using a mold or small paper cups and Popsicle sticks. Fill with fruit juice, fruit chunks, blended yogurt and fruit, or pudding. Freeze and enjoy!

# Frozen Banana Parfait

1 banana, peeled and frozen (place in sealable bag or
   wrap with plastic wrap to freeze)
Ice cream flavor of choice
Whipped cream
Chocolate chips

Remove the banana from the freezer and allow to thaw a
few minutes. Slice the banana into 1/8- to 1/4-inch pieces.
Layer an individual bowl with ice cream and banana slices,
and top with a generous portion of whipped cream. Sprinkle chocolate chips over the top and enjoy!

**Makes 1 parfait.**

- - - - -  **Variation**  - - - - -

Peel the banana and insert a Popsicle stick into the end.
Wrap and freeze. When frozen, unwrap the banana and dip
it into some Luscious Chocolate Sauce (see page 192).

# Luscious Chocolate Sauce

*Use this satisfying sauce over cake, frozen yogurt,*
*fresh fruit, or ice cream.*

1/2 cup unrefined sugar
1/2 cup unsweetened cocoa
1 cup nonfat milk
1 tablespoon butter
1/4 cup semisweet chocolate chips
1 teaspoon real vanilla extract

Combine the sugar, cocoa, milk, and butter in a small
saucepan and stir. Bring to a boil over medium heat, stirring
constantly. Use a wire whisk to smooth out clumps of cocoa
if necessary. Remove from heat and stir in chocolate chips
and vanilla, stirring until chocolate melts. Serve warm or let
stand 10 minutes to thicken.

**Serves 12.**

### Variation

Add 2 tablespoons of Kahlua, Grand Marnier, or a coffee
liqueur to the chocolate sauce at the end of cooking.

Use organic milk when possible, or substitute soy milk, which is a nice alternative for those who want to avoid dairy milk.

# Chocolate Chip Pan Cookies

*This is an RV version of our favorite chocolate chip cookies. No baking soda or baking powder are necessary, and there is no long wait for several pans of cookies to bake. These smell heavenly as they bake!*

3/4 cup (1 1/2 sticks) butter*
1 cup unrefined cane sugar (or honey or barley malt sweetener)
1 tablespoon vanilla extract
2 eggs
2 cups whole wheat flour
1/2 teaspoon salt or sea salt
1/2 to 1 package chocolate chips
1 cup walnuts

Preheat the oven to 375 degrees F. Mix the butter, sugar, vanilla, and eggs together in a large mixing bowl. Add the flour and salt and mix well. Add the chocolate chips (1/2 package of chips does the trick—use more if desired) and walnuts and mix until the dough holds together. Drop the dough into a shallow baking dish. Press the dough in firmly with a spoon or your fingers and bake for 20 minutes. Check it frequently as all ovens bake at slightly different temperatures, and elevations can change baking time. Serve hot or let cool and cut into bars for a picnic.

**Makes 8 cookies.**

*Use butter at room temperature, or if butter is cold and hard, use a cheese grater to grate the sticks of butter.

Save butter wrappers and use them to grease a baking dish before you throw them away.

Use whole wheat flour in place of white flour because whole grain flours contain beneficial fiber and vitamin E.

# Apple Crisp

5 large tart apples
Cooking spray
1 tablespoon vanilla extract
1/4 cup sugar
Topping (follows)
Vanilla ice cream or whipped cream

Preheat the oven to 350 degrees F. Peel, core, and slice the apples and place them in a baking pan sprayed with cooking spray. Sprinkle the vanilla extract and sugar over the apples. Sprinkle the topping mixture on top of the apples and cover the pan with foil. Bake covered for 30 minutes, then remove the foil and bake an additional 20 minutes to brown the topping. Serve warm. Top warm apple crisp with a scoop of vanilla ice cream or a dollop of whipped cream.

### Topping
1 teaspoon cinnamon or pumpkin pie spice
1 1/2 cups whole wheat flour
1/2 cup rolled oats
3/4 cup firmly packed brown sugar
1/2 cup (1 stick) butter, softened

In a small bowl, mix together all ingredients until crumbly.

**Serves 4 to 6.**

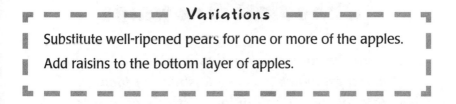

**Variations**

Substitute well-ripened pears for one or more of the apples.

Add raisins to the bottom layer of apples.

To soften the butter for this recipe, simply place the butter in a small saucepan on the stove and warm for a few minutes on low. Use the saucepan as a mixing bowl for the preparation of the topping . . . one less bowl to clean!

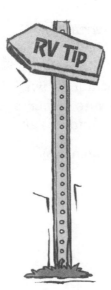

# Chocolate Brownies

*The muffin tin version makes individual brownie*
*servings, which are easy to share on picnics.*
*Chocolate lovers will fall in love with these easy-to-make*
*decadent treats—they're great with ice cream!*

1/2 cup (1 stick) butter, softened
1 cup sugar
3/4 cup cocoa powder
2 eggs
1 cup unbleached wheat flour

Preheat the oven to 350 degrees F. Blend the butter and sugar together in a medium bowl. Mix in the remaining ingredients and spoon into either a baking dish or muffin tins. Bake for 10 to 12 minutes and serve warm.

**Makes 9 little cakes (in muffin tins).**

# Katie's Dutch Babies

1/4 cup (1/2 stick) butter

3 eggs

3/4 cup milk

3/4 cup flour

Lemon, powdered sugar, fruit, maple syrup, cinnamon
   (optional)

Preheat the oven to 425 degrees F. While oven is preheating, melt the butter in a shallow baking dish or an oven-safe skillet in the oven. In a large bowl, combine the eggs, milk, and flour and whip together with a fork or wire whisk to break up all the lumps of flour. Remove the pan from the oven and pour the batter into the hot melted butter. Bake until fluffy and well browned, 20 to 25 minutes. Serve at once with lemon, powdered sugar, fruit, maple syrup, cinnamon, or any topping you desire.

**Serves 6.**

This recipe works just as well with lowfat or nonfat milk. Top with generous servings of fresh fruit to add nutrients.

Use a blender to make the batter even fluffier.

# Chocolate Pudding

1/2 cup chocolate chips
2 boxes (12.3 ounces) silken firm tofu (organic)
3 tablespoons water

Melt the chocolate chips in the microwave or on the stove-top. As soon as they hit their melting point, scrape them into the blender and add the tofu and water. Whip them up until the mixture is smooth and creamy. Pour the mixture into a prebaked pie shell or serving dishes and serve immediately, or chill and serve later.

**Serves 4.**

To make blender cleanup a snap, fill it halfway with warm water and add a drop of dish soap. Blend on high for 30 seconds, then wash as usual. Less mess!

Mori Nu brand tofu comes in aseptic boxes that do not require refrigeration. Buy the organic tofu to avoid agricultural chemical residue.

# Almond Tapioca

1 egg
$1/3$ cup unrefined sugar
3 tablespoons instant tapioca
3 cups lowfat or nonfat milk
$1/2$ teaspoon vanilla extract
$1/2$ teaspoon almond extract
$1/2$ cup sliced almonds

In a medium saucepan, beat the egg and mix in the sugar, tapioca, and milk. Let stand for 5 minutes, then heat it on the stove over medium, stirring constantly, until mixture comes to a boil. Remove from heat and stir in the vanilla and almond extracts. Place in the refrigerator to cool for at least 20 minutes. Stir in the almonds just before serving.

**Serves 4.**

Keep a box of instant nonfat milk powder on hand. It replaces liquid milk in any recipe and has a much longer shelf life. It is easy to reconstitute by simply following the directions on the box for milk powder to water ratios.

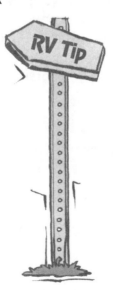

# Easy Cheesecake

*Amy's mom, Bobbie, loves to make this dessert, as it is so easy to prepare and is always a crowd pleaser!*

1 pound lowfat cream cheese
3 eggs
2/3 cup sugar
1 teaspoon almond extract
Topping (follows)
Slivered almonds, fresh blueberries, or fresh strawberries
   (optional)

Preheat the oven to 350 degrees F. Blend together the cream cheese, eggs, sugar, and almond extract until creamy. Pour the mixture into a greased or nonstick 9-inch pie pan. Bake for 25 minutes. Remove the pie from the oven after 25 minutes and let cool for 10 minutes. After cooling, pour the topping over the pie, allowing 1/2 inch around the edge of the pie to remain uncovered. Place in the oven for an additional 10 minutes. Remove from the oven and cool or refrigerate before serving. Garnish the baked pie with slivered almonds, fresh blueberries, or fresh strawberries, if desired.

### Topping
1 cup lowfat sour cream
2 tablespoons sugar
1 1/2 teaspoons vanilla

Mix all ingredients in a small bowl and set aside.

**Makes 1 cheesecake.**

This is the simplest cheesecake recipe, as it requires no crust or springform pan, yet it has all the flavor and creaminess we love. Make this for dessert and you'll be sure to impress your fellow RVers!

RV Tip

Nutrition Tip

For a lower calorie dessert, use nonfat cream cheese and/or substitute the sour cream used in the topping with lowfat plain yogurt.

# Gingerbread

$1/2$ cup (1 stick) butter
1 cup dark molasses
1 egg
1 cup orange juice
$2^1/2$ cups unbleached flour
1 teaspoon baking soda
2 teaspoons cinnamon
3 teaspoons powdered ginger
$1/2$ teaspoon salt
1 tablespoon orange zest
Ice cream or whipped cream

Preheat the oven to 350 degrees F. Soften the butter in a large saucepan over low heat. Using the saucepan as a mixing bowl, add the molasses, egg, and orange juice to the butter. Blend well. In a separate bowl, mix the flour, baking soda, cinnamon, ginger, salt, and orange zest. Add the dry ingredients to the wet and mix well. Pour the batter into an oven-safe baking dish and bake for 40 minutes. Serve warm with ice cream or whipped cream.

**Serves 8.**

Coat your measuring cup with spray oil before measuring molasses. The molasses will slide out easily, and cleanup will be a snap!

Use Black Strap Molasses, as it is a rich source of the mineral iron—an essential nutrient for women.

# Cinnamon Peach Tart

6 puff pastry shells*
2 cans (15 ounces each) sliced peaches, packed in juice,
   drained and chopped into small pieces
2 tablespoons sugar
1 teaspoon cinnamon
1 tablespoon flour
1 teaspoon lemon juice
Vanilla ice cream (optional)

Bake the pastry shells according to the directions on the box. While the pastry shells are baking, add the peaches, sugar, cinnamon, flour, and lemon juice to a small saucepan and heat over medium for 5 minutes. When the pastry shells are finished baking, remove the caps according to the directions and set aside. Fill the pastry shells with the peach mixture, leaving any leftover amount in the saucepan. Place the pastry caps on top of the peach mixture and return to the oven for 5 minutes. Serve these tarts hot out of the oven. Place a peach tart in a small bowl, adding a scoop of vanilla ice cream topped with leftover peach mixture.

*Puff pastry is sold in the frozen foods section of most grocery stores. For this recipe, choose the variety sold in a box of 6 pastry shells. The pastry shells start out as flat disks and rise up as they are baked. For best results, always follow the directions on the package.

**Makes 6 tarts.**

## Variation

Add 1/2 cup chopped walnuts to the peach mixture to add protein and a nutty texture.

Save the juice from the canned peaches, freezing it in ice cube trays for later use. Jazz up a glass of sparkling water or a cocktail with these flavorful frozen juice cubes, or toss them into the blender as part of a fruit smoothie recipe.

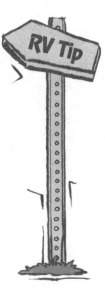

# CHAPTER 16

# Exotic Elixirs

## Hot and Cold Beverages

 Quench your thirst with refreshing summer beverages. Warm your spirit with hot rum drinks. There's something for everyone and every season in this chapter!

# Hibiscus-Cranberry Cooler

*This refreshing drink is low in calories, as it
combines herbal tea with juice for a delicious,
light drink for both kids and adults.*

2 bags Celestial Seasonings Red Zinger herbal tea
2 cups boiling water
2 cups cranberry juice blend
1 cup cold water
Lemon or lime slices (optional)

In a heatproof pitcher, steep the tea bags in boiling water
for 10 minutes. Remove the tea bags and add the cranberry
juice blend and cold water. Stir well, chill, and serve with a
slice of lemon or lime.

**Serves 4.**

Knudsen's cranberry concentrate
comes in a small bottle. Add
water to the liquid concentrate
to make a pitcher of juice.

Choose a variety of cran-
berry juice that has no
sugar added. There
are many varieties
available, including
cranberry-raspberry,
cranberry-grape, and
cranberry-apple.

# Hot Toddy

*Amy's dad, Dick, whose creative talents include a flair
for wonderful beverage concoctions, inspired this drink.*

1¹/₄ cups orange juice
2 teaspoons lemon juice
2 teaspoons honey
¹/₄ teaspoon cinnamon
1 shot dark rum

Mix the orange juice, lemon juice, honey, and cinnamon in
a small saucepan and heat over low. When the liquid is hot
but not yet boiling, add the rum and turn off heat. Pour
into a large mug and drink hot.

**Serves 1.**

# Swamp Water

*This recipe was inspired by our friends the Westbrooks, owners of the world's best barbecue joint, Grandpa's BBQ, in Arco, Idaho. You must stop in and sample Lloyd and Loretta's authentic Southern fare if you're in the area! This simple, refreshing drink is made by combining equal parts pink lemonade with unsweetened iced tea. Experiment to find what proportions suit your taste.*

2 cups iced tea
2 cups lemonade

Combine and chill for a light, refreshing summer drink.

**Serves 4.**

Make a decaffeinated version with decaf tea bags or herbal tea, if you prefer.

# Karim's Lime Spritzer

Juice of 4 limes
$^{1}/_3$ cup brown sugar
$^{1}/_4$ cup mint leaves
1-inch stick ginger, peeled
1 bottle (1 liter) sparkling water

Combine all the ingredients in a pitcher, stirring well to blend the flavors. Drink immediately or make a few hours in advance and refrigerate. This will allow the flavors to mingle, resulting in a more potent lime taste.

**Serves 10.**

# Warm Maple Soother

*The blending of maple syrup and vanilla with a hint
of rum create a decadent, warming drink.*

1 cup nonfat or lowfat milk
1 tablespoon real maple syrup
1/2 teaspoon real vanilla flavoring
1 shot rum

In a small saucepan, heat the milk until warm (do not boil).
Remove from heat and stir in the maple syrup, vanilla, and
rum. Mix well and pour into an individual serving mug.
Drink while hot.

**Serves 1.**

# Orange Sherbet Cup

*This recipe is from* Smoothies for Life *by Daniella Chace
and Maureen Keane (Prima Publishing, 1998).
This drink makes a nice breakfast, snack, or dessert.*

1 cup nonfat or lowfat milk
1/2 cup nonfat or lowfat vanilla yogurt
1/2 cup orange sherbet
1 teaspoon vitamin C powder (optional)
1 teaspoon lecithin (optional)

Place all the ingredients in a blender and whip until smooth
and creamy. Serve immediately.

**Serves 1.**

# Spiced Cider with Orange Slices

*A wonderful warming drink to enjoy by the campfire on a cool fall evening.*

2 cups unsweetened cider
1/4 teaspoon cinnamon
1/4 teaspoon ginger
2 teaspoons honey
1 orange
1/4 teaspoon orange zest (from orange rind)

In a small saucepan, heat the cider over low. Add the cinnamon, ginger, and honey, stirring well. Grate the orange rind and add to the liquid for zest. Peel half of the orange, squeezing juice from the unpeeled half into the cider mixture. Cut the peeled orange half into thin slices and place in the bottom of each of 2 mugs. Continue to heat the cider on low for 3 to 5 minutes. When finished, pour the cider over the orange slices in the mugs. Serve hot.

**Serves 2.**

# Lemon-Lime Margarita

*This extra-tangy drink combines the tartness of lemons and limes. It's a great summer refresher!*

Coarsely ground sea salt
1 shot tequila
1 shot triple sec
1 shot Rose's lime juice
1 teaspoon fresh lemon juice
Shaved ice

Wet the rim of each glass and dip it into the salt. Combine the tequila, triple sec, lime juice, and lemon juice, add shaved ice, and stir.

**Serves 1.**

**Nutrition Tip**

Emer'gen-C packets are available at most health food stores and grocery stores. They make great drinks for a hot day and give you an energy boost, plus vitamin C and lots of other important nutrients. Perfect for hot weather hiking. Just add the packet to your water bottle and drink to replace lost electrolytes and water in your body.

# Kahlua Cocoa

2 packets instant cocoa mix
2 cups hot water
4 tablespoons liqueur (Kahlua, Bailey's Irish Cream, etc.)

Put each packet of hot cocoa mix separately into 2 cups hot water to make 2 cups of hot cocoa. Add 2 tablespoons of Kahlua or Bailey's Irish Cream to each cup for an adult version of the classic chocolate drink.

**Serves 2.**

# Wine Spritzer

¹/₂ cup white wine
¹/₄ cup fruit juice (cranberry, pineapple, mango, etc.)
¹/₄ cup seltzer water

Combine all the ingredients in a large glass. Serve with ice cubes or cubes of frozen juice.

**Serves 1.**

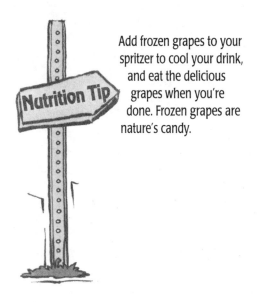

Add frozen grapes to your spritzer to cool your drink, and eat the delicious grapes when you're done. Frozen grapes are nature's candy.

# Glossary

**Al dente:** An Italian term that means "to the tooth." It usually refers to pasta and vegetables, and indicates that food is cooked just enough to retain a somewhat firm texture.

**Aseptic box:** Shelf-stable boxes that do not require refrigeration until they are opened, usually containing soy milk, grain milks, and juices. They are handy for picnics and long trips because they are unbreakable and stack and store easily; they are ideal for RVers.

**Baked tofu:** Tofu comes in a variety of forms (see Tofu). Baked tofu products are so tasty they require no added spices. They can be eaten straight from the package, used on sandwiches or to top salads, or added to dishes and heated.

**Balsamic vinegar:** Italian vinegar that is aged over many years in wooden vats and has a sweet, rich flavor. Combined with olive oil and lemon juice, it is a refreshing summer salad dressing.

**Barley malt syrup:** Sweetener that is made from sprouted barley grains and has a rich malt flavor that lends itself well to cookies and baking. It can be used instead of sugar in most recipes.

**Basmati rice:** A long-grain aromatic rice with a delicate flavor that is perfect for salads and pilafs.

**Blood sugar:** Those with diabetes or hypoglycemia are constantly working to stabilize their blood sugar. In other words, they are trying to keep the amount of sugar in their bloodstreams at a low level for health reasons. Reducing the amount of sugar in the diet is the primary way to achieve this, so we have kept sugar to a minimum where possible in recipes.

**Brown rice syrup:** A syrup that is less refined than table sugar and contains many of the nutrients of brown rice. It is a less-sweet alternative to white sugar in baking.

**Cajun blackened seasoning:** A seasoning mix that is quick to use and takes up less room than having an entire rack of individual spices in your RV kitchen. The cayenne pepper in Cajun seasoning imparts a hot, zesty flavor to fish, meat, and vegetable dishes.

**Canola oil:** The advantage of canola oil is that it has a high smoking point, which means that it can be heated to higher temperatures than most oils without burning. Never ingest burnt oils as they contain free radicals that are unhealthy. Canola does not have much flavor and is best kept for this purpose alone. Buy organic oils when possible.

**Cayenne:** A spice containing hot red chili peppers (cayenne pepper) that can be purchased whole (fresh or dried) or powdered. The cayenne pepper's active oil is called capsicum, and it helps improve circulation. Cayenne adds heat to soups, stews, dips, meat rubs, dressings, and sautés.

**Cilantro:** Cilantro leaves come from the coriander plant and are also known as Chinese parsley. They are sold fresh in the produce department of grocery stores and dried in the spice section. They have a distinct aroma and taste that adds fresh Mexican flavor to burritos, nachos, and soups.

**Cocoa powder:** A dry residue that is produced after cocoa beans have had the cocoa butter removed. It is sold for baking and making drinking chocolate.

**Coconut milk:** This is not the clear liquid inside the coconut but the liquid extracted from the grated coconut flesh. It is available in coconut cream (thick), which is from the first extraction, or milk (thin), which is the second extraction. It is also available in a lowfat variety, which has a considerably lower fat content and tastes just as good. It is sweet and nutty in flavor and adds a creamy texture to curry dishes and desserts.

**Couscous:** A pasta made from semolina that is available in its traditional longer-cooking form and an instant form that takes about 5 minutes to cook.

**Cranberry juice:** Cranberry juice is used by millions of women to keep urinary tract infections at bay. Just 1 glass of juice a day does the trick for most women.

**Curry powder:** Powder that is made from varying combinations of the following spices: ground turmeric, cumin, coriander, cardamom, chili, fennel seeds, cloves, fenugreek, tamarind, poppy seeds, saffron, pepper, nutmeg, mace, garlic, and ginger. Curry powder can be added to mayonnaise and used to coat cold pasta or added to coconut milk and poured over vegetables and rice for a quick exotic dish.

**Deveined:** To remove the black line (digestive parts) of the shrimp. This is done by cutting a slit along the outside length of the shrimp with a sharp knife or deveining tool and removing the dark threadlike piece before cooking the shrimp. This is generally not necessary for smaller shrimp. However, large shrimp may have gritty material in the tract, and removal may be preferred.

**Dice:** A term that refers to cutting pieces that are not as fine as a mince but not as coarse as a chop.

**Flaxseed:** Whole flaxseeds, ground flaxseeds, and flax oil are sold in most grocery stores and natural food markets. They can be added to cereals and baked goods but should be ground to first release their oils. They contain vital essential fatty acids, which have powerful medicinal benefits including anti-inflammatory action and hormone stabilization. Flaxseed can be ground in a coffee grinder or blender or purchased preground. Once ground, it must be stored in the refrigerator or freezer or the oils will become rancid. If the ground seed or oil smells fishy rather than fresh and nutty, it is rancid and should be disposed of.

**Hot chili oil:** Strong volatile oils of red chilies that are extracted and sold in the Asian section of most grocery stores. A small amount will add zest to sauces, salsas, dips, and sautéed vegetables.

**Imitation crabmeat:** This product is less expensive than actual crabmeat but tastes very similar. It is made from the fish pollock or a combination of pollock and Pacific whiting.

**Italian seasoning:** A common herb mix that contains marjoram, thyme, rosemary, savory, sage, oregano, and basil. It's a nice combination for sauces, pizza, dips, and even eggs.

**Julienne:** To cut into fine, even pieces that look like matchsticks.

**Kalamata olive:** Greek olives that are preserved in either salt and citric acid or in olive oil. Buy the pitted olives if you don't want the chore of removing the pits.

**Lecithin:** Also known as phosphatidylcholine, this product can be added to baked goods to give them a creamier texture. It also has the health benefit of protecting arteries from cholesterol buildup. Some experts believe that lecithin is also helpful in treating neurological disorders, senility, arthritis, and liver problems. Lecithin is found in both granulated and liquid form. It looks like millet but is more waxy or oily in appearance. It is sold in most grocery stores and natural food markets.

**Lecithin granules:** See Lecithin.

**Mince:** To finely chop into smaller pieces than a dice.

**Nonfat milk powder:** An ingredient that can be reconstituted to make milk on the spur of the moment or added to smoothies to increase the protein content.

**Olive oil, extra virgin:** The highest quality olive oil, denoting the very first pressing, which requires no chemicals for extraction. The term "organic" means that the olives were grown without chemical fertilizers, herbicides, or pesticides and that the plants were not genetically engineered.

**Olive tapenade:** A Mediterranean dish of chopped olives, garlic, and herbs. It is pronounced "top-n-nod" and is traditionally served on crusty bread with wine.

**Omega-3 fatty acids:** Part of the oils that are found naturally occurring in fish. Some vegetarian sources of these oils are flax oil, nuts, and seeds. These oils are essential to good health.

**Organic:** A term that designates that a product, produce, or an animal product was grown without chemical fertilizers, herbicides, or pesticides and was not genetically engineered in any way. Choose organic products whenever possible.

**Oyster sauce:** A pungent sauce that is sweet and salty and made from oysters. It is a common ingredient in Chinese dishes from noodles to vegetables. It should be refrigerated after opening.

**Pesto:** Pesto sauce is traditionally made from fresh basil leaves, olive oil, garlic, and pine nuts. New pesto variations include spinach and arugula, and walnuts may replace the pine nuts. Pesto is used as a spread for sandwiches, served on crackers with fresh tomato slices, or mixed with pasta and served either hot or cold.

**Polenta:** This meal or flour is made from yellow and white corn. Mixed with water and brought to a boil, it cooks into a porridge-like consistency. Polenta can be eaten hot or cooled and then sliced into pieces, which are then fried or grilled.

**Potato flakes:** There are many freeze-dried vegetables now available either packaged or in the bulk department of most grocery stores. Potato flakes can be reconstituted with hot water. They are lightweight, inexpensive, taste great, and take just minutes to make.

**Pressure cooker:** A handy kitchen tool that dramatically reduces cooking time for longer-cooking foods such as beans, meat, and some grains. Meat dishes such as pot roast, and root vegetables such as potatoes, cook in just minutes.

**Puff pastry:** Ready-made pastry shells or sheets of dough found in the freezer section of the grocery store. When kept frozen, they last for months, so you'll have them on hand for making a quick gourmet meal anywhere. They can be made into pot pies, filled with sweet fruit for desserts, or filled with dip and served as an appetizer. Because hydrogenated fats are unhealthy, you should buy products low in hydrogenated oils whenever possible.

**Pumpkin pie spice:** A mix that contains nutmeg, cinnamon, ginger, and allspice.

**Red curry paste:** Curry is available in powder or paste form. There are several exceptional curry pastes now available in the Asian import section of many grocery stores. The pastes are handy because they mix easily into pasta, grains, or vegetable or meat dishes.

**Refried beans:** Generally, refried beans are made from pinto beans, but they can be made from any bean. They are either sold dried, which can easily be reconstituted with hot water, or purchased in a can, ready to eat. They are high in protein and sold in lowfat, nonfat, low-sodium, vegetarian, and spicy versions. These are good to have on hand to make quick burritos.

**Sauté:** Rapid cooking over medium–high heat in oil until browned.

**Sea salt:** Sea salt grains are the natural crystals of evaporated sea water, as opposed to table salt, which is mined out of the ground. Sea salt has a higher mineral content and many feel it has a better flavor than table salt. It comes as fine, coarse, or flaky crystals. Be sure to buy sea salt with iodine added. Iodized salt is one of the few dietary sources of this essential trace mineral.

**Sesame oil:** An oil with a toasted flavor that is delicious in Asian pastas, stir-fries, and dressings. Sesame oil is available in raw or toasted flavors and should be kept in the refrigerator to extend its life.

**Skewer:** Long sticklike tools that usually hold chunks of vegetables and meats for easy cooking over a fire or barbecue. Many skewers (available in kitchen stores) are made from bamboo. These skewers must be soaked in water before use so they won't burn and catch on fire. The steel skewers are made in many lengths and work the best.

**Soy analogs:** Vegetarian products made from soybeans that resemble, both in look and taste, specific meat, cheese, and dairy products. There is a wide range of meat alternatives on the market today including names such as Veggie Ground Round and Gimme Lean Sausage. Replacements for pepperoni, hamburger, sausage, lunch meat, cheeses, and milks are available, and even the most staunch of meat lovers will enjoy these tasty and high-protein alternatives.

**Soy milk:** Milk products that are made from soybeans and are available in every variety that dairy milk comes in, including 1 percent, 2 percent, whole fat, chocolate, vanilla, eggnog flavor, and dried milk powder. The powder can be used to add protein to smoothies or pancakes, and other baking batters.

**Soy sauce:** A fermented soybean sauce that is salty and pungent and the key to many Asian dishes and dressings. If you want to reduce sodium in your diet, try the reduced sodium version of this favorite condiment. Tamari is a very similar product found in the same section of the grocery store, but it has a sweeter flavor (see Tamari). We prefer tamari to soy sauce, but they can be used interchangeably in all of our recipes.

**Soybean:** Young, green soybeans also known as edamame when steamed. Soybeans are so nutritious and versatile that many whole forms and products are now widely available. Whole mature beans can be cooked and used as you would any other variety of dry bean to make soups and stews. Soy nuts are roasted versions of soybeans and sold as snack food.

**Spike seasoning:** A powdered spice mix available in most grocery stores in the United States and Canada. It's a versatile mix of salt and more than 20 different seasonings.

**Sun-dried tomatoes:** These can be found in jars of olive oil in many markets, but RVers may want to look for dried tomatoes because they weigh very little, require no refrigeration, and can be reconstituted in water. Add these to pasta, sandwiches, and vegetable dishes for a Mediterranean flair.

**Tahini:** The paste of ground sesame seeds. Toasted sesame seed tahini is also available and has a richer flavor. This paste is the key ingredient in many Middle Eastern dips and sauces such as hummus.

**Tamari:** A variety of soy sauce (see Soy Sauce). It is a salty sauce used in the same dishes as soy sauce but it is sweeter in flavor and is available in a wheat-free variety for those who are avoiding all wheat and wheat-containing products.

**Tofu:** Soybean curd is made into an array of tofu products. It is flavorless on its own but absorbs spices, oils, and flavors well. It is high in protein and healthy fat and is often used to replace meat in traditional American fare.

**Vitamin C powder:** The antioxidant vitamin C is available in many powdered forms that can be added to liquid to make a refreshing elixir that protects the immune system and helps stave off colds.

**Wheat germ:** Grains have a component called germ, which is the part of the plant that contains its fat-soluble vitamins such as vitamins D and E. Wheat germ can be purchased in bags and stored in the freezer, then added to cereals, baking, and smoothies to add a bit of fiber and nutrients.

**Worcestershire sauce:** A spicy sauce made from a combination of several of the following ingredients: mushrooms, walnuts, vinegar, salt, soy sauce, sugar, tamarind, peppers, spices, garlic, and anchovies. It's famous for its use in the drink Bloody Mary, and it is often sprinkled over cooked meats.

**Zest:** The result of scraping the outer peel of oranges and lemons to release the volatile oils in the skin, which impart a fresh citrus flavor to drinks, baked goods, and sauces.

# Resources

## Natural Food Stores

In our travels we've discovered a number of natural food grocery store chains with exceptional products from bulk foods and organic produce to nontoxic cleaning supplies and extraordinary kitchen equipment. You will find these wonderful stores across the United States and Canada:

Puget Consumer's Co-ops (Washington State)
Whole Foods Markets
Fresh Fields
Wild Oats
Trader Joe's

Additionally, look for small, independently owned and operated food co-ops and natural food stores in your travels when you need to stock your pantry with bulk foods and supplies.

## General RV Information

There are many helpful resources available to the RVer—from magazines and Web sites to clubs and directories. To simplify this wealth of information, we encourage you to do a bit of Web surfing. Customize your search or head straight to www.rvusa.com, a site designed to provide RVers with just about everything they need to locate RV parts, accessories, magazines, clubs, maps, and so much more.

## Our Favorite Equipment

We'd like to take a moment to brag about two of our favorite kitchen equipment companies. Both OXO and Zyliss provided us with an array of kitchen tools to assist us in our recipe testing. As you equip your RV kitchen with the essentials, we encourage you to look for the wonderful tools from OXO and Zyliss, as so many of them are perfectly suited to the RV lifestyle. You'll be pleased with both the quality and design!

# Index

# International Conversion Chart

These are not exact equivalents: they have been slightly rounded to make measuring easier.

## LIQUID MEASUREMENTS

| American | Imperial | Metric | Australian |
|---|---|---|---|
| 2 tablespoons (1 oz.) | 1 fl. oz. | 30 ml | 1 tablespoon |
| ¼ cup (2 oz.) | 2 fl. oz. | 60 ml | 2 tablespoons |
| ⅓ cup (3 oz.) | 3 fl. oz. | 80 ml | ¼ cup |
| ½ cup (4 oz.) | 4 fl. oz. | 125 ml | ⅓ cup |
| ⅔ cup (5 oz.) | 5 fl. oz. | 165 ml | ½ cup |
| ¾ cup (6 oz.) | 6 fl. oz. | 185 ml | ⅔ cup |
| 1 cup (8 oz.) | 8 fl. oz. | 250 ml | ¾ cup |

## SPOON MEASUREMENTS

| American | Metric |
|---|---|
| ¼ teaspoon | 1 ml |
| ½ teaspoon | 2 ml |
| 1 teaspoon | 5 ml |
| 1 tablespoon | 15 ml |

## WEIGHTS

| US/UK | Metric |
|---|---|
| 1 oz. | 30 grams (g) |
| 2 oz. | 60 g |
| 4 oz. (¼ lb) | 125 g |
| 5 oz. (⅓ lb) | 155 g |
| 6 oz. | 185 g |
| 7 oz. | 220 g |
| 8 oz. (½ lb) | 250 g |
| 10 oz. | 315 g |
| 12 oz. (¾ lb) | 375 g |
| 14 oz. | 440 g |
| 16 oz. (1 lb) | 500 g |
| 2 lbs | 1 kg |

## OVEN TEMPERATURES

| Farenheit | Centigrade | Gas |
|---|---|---|
| 250 | 120 | ¼ |
| 300 | 150 | 2 |
| 325 | 160 | 3 |
| 350 | 180 | 4 |
| 375 | 190 | 5 |
| 400 | 200 | 6 |
| 450 | 230 | 8 |

# About the Authors

**Amy Boyer** (right) left her fast-paced life behind when she and her husband, Dean, sold their home in Pennsylvania, packed their VW Eurovan camper, and hit the road. After a year-and-a-half of travel and adventure throughout the United States and Canada, they settled in Hailey, Idaho, where they live with their new dog, Sailor, and two cats. Whether she's in the great outdoors or in her kitchen at home, Amy enjoys creating meals for her family and friends that nourish both body and soul.

**Daniella Chace** (left) is a nutritionist and has a bachelor's degree in Natural Health Sciences and a master's degree in nutrition from Bastyr University in Seattle, Washington. She lives in Hailey, Idaho, where she teaches cooking classes and workshops on various health and nutrition topics. Daniella is almost always researching or writing, and is the author of over 13 nutrition books. She is currently investigating the health and environmental effects of genetically altered foods, thus her passion for organic foods. She loves to adventure whenever possible, as long as fabulous food is involved in the excursion!